WHAT IS THE BOOK OF 1 KINGS?

Kids' Guides to God's Word Series

What Is the Book of Genesis?
What Is the Book of Exodus?
What Is the Book of Leviticus?
What Is the Book of Numbers?
What Is the Book of Deuteronomy?
What Is the Book of Joshua?
What Is the Book of Judges?
What Is the Book of Ruth?
What Is the Book of 1 Samuel?
What Is the Book of 2 Samuel?
What Is the Book of 1 Kings?
What Is the Book of 2 Kings?
What Are the Books of 1–2 Chronicles?
What Are the Books of Ezra & Nehemiah?
What Is the Book of Esther?
What Is the Book of Job?
What Is the Book of Psalms?
What Is the Book of Proverbs?
What Is the Book of Ecclesiastes?
What Are the Books of Song of Songs & Lamentations?
What Is the Book of Isaiah?
What Is the Book of Jeremiah?
What Is the Book of Ezekiel?
What Is the Book of Daniel?
What Are the Books of Hosea–Micah?
What Are the Books of Nahum–Malachi?
What Is the Gospel of Matthew?
What Is the Gospel of Mark?
What Is the Gospel of Luke?
What Is the Gospel of John?
What Is the Book of Acts?
What Is the Book of Romans?
What Is the Book of 1 Corinthians?
What Is the Book of 2 Corinthians?
What Is the Book of Galatians?
What Is the Book of Ephesians?
What Is the Book of Philippians?
What Are the Books of Colossians & Philemon?
What Are the Books of 1–2 Thessalonians?
What Are the Books of 1–2 Timothy & Titus?
What Is the Book of Hebrews?
What Is the Book of James?
What Are the Books of 1–2 Peter & Jude?
What Are the Books of 1-3 John?
What Is the Book of Revelation?

What Is the Book of

1 KINGS?

Michael Whitworth

ISBN 978-1-971767-17-8

Published by Start2Finish
Bend, Oregon 97702
start2finish.org

Printed in the United States of America

30 29 28 27 26 1 2 3 4 5

CONTENTS

INTRODUCTION

What would you do if the smartest person who ever lived made the dumbest decision imaginable? That's not a riddle. It's the story of 1 Kings.

This book starts with a golden age. Israel is united, powerful, and at peace. A king named Solomon builds the most spectacular building in the ancient world—a temple for God that takes seven years and more wealth than you can imagine. He's so wise that foreign rulers travel thousands of miles just to hear him talk. His kingdom stretches from the Euphrates River to the border of Egypt. For one shining moment, everything God promised Abraham centuries earlier seems to be coming true.

And then Solomon starts collecting foreign wives—seven hundred of them, plus three hundred concubines—and they turn his heart toward other gods. The wisest man who ever lived bows down to idols. And everything falls apart.

That's just the first eleven chapters.

By the end of 1 Kings, the united kingdom has been ripped in two. The northern kingdom of Israel has cycled through dynasty after dynasty, each one more corrupt than the last. A king named Ahab and his queen Jezebel have dragged the nation into full-blown Baal worship. Prophets are being hunted down and killed. And the man who stands on a mountaintop and calls fire from heaven spends the next chapter lying under a bush in the desert, begging God to let him die.

First Kings is wild. And it matters more than you might think.

WHY 1 KINGS MATTERS

If you've been reading through the Old Testament story, you know how we got here. God called Abraham and promised him a land, a nation, and a blessing. That family went to Egypt, became slaves, and was rescued by God through Moses. Joshua led them into the promised land. The book of Judges showed what happened when everyone did what was right in their own eyes: chaos, cruelty, and a desperate need for real leadership. Ruth gave us a quiet story of faithfulness in the middle of that darkness. Then came Samuel, Saul, and finally David, the king after God's own heart, the one God promised would establish a dynasty that would never end.

First Kings picks up right where that story left off. David is old and dying. The question hanging over everything is: What will happen to God's promises now?

The answer, it turns out, is complicated. God's promises don't fail, but his people do. Over and over again. First Kings is the story of how a kingdom that had everything managed to lose almost all of it, and what God did in the middle of that disaster.

This book matters because it forces you to wrestle with questions that are just as real today as they were three thousand years ago. Can smart people make terrible choices? (Yes.) Does God give up on people who fail him? (No.) What happens when an entire culture decides that God's word doesn't matter anymore? (Nothing good.) Is it possible to stand for the truth when everyone around you is going the other direction? (Yes, but it costs you something.)

First Kings also introduces us to some of the most unforgettable characters in the entire Bible. Solomon, the brilliant king who couldn't control his own heart. Rehoboam, the young fool who split a nation with a single speech. Jeroboam, the rebel king who invented a new religion for political convenience. Elijah, the prophet who appeared out of nowhere to challenge an empire. Jezebel, the queen who made evil into a government program. And Ahab, the king who was so weak that his passivity became its own kind of wickedness.

These aren't dusty historical figures. They're mirrors. You'll recognize people you know—and, if you're honest, yourself—in almost every chapter.

WHAT YOU'RE ABOUT TO READ

Here's a quick roadmap of where we're headed. The book opens with the end of David's reign and the rise of Solomon (chapters 1–2). It's a messy transition involving rival claims to the throne, political maneuvering, and the settling of old scores. David's final words to Solomon are a mix of spiritual wisdom and political hardball.

The next section covers Solomon's glory (chapters 3–10). This is the high point of the entire Old Testament story. Solomon asks God for wisdom and receives it. He builds the temple and dedicates it with a prayer that still echoes through Scripture. The kingdom reaches a level of prosperity and international prestige it will never see again. Foreign leaders come bearing gifts. The wealth is staggering. It looks like the dream is finally real.

Then comes the fall (chapter 11). Solomon's foreign wives turn his heart to other gods. God tells him the kingdom will be torn from his son's hand. The cracks begin to show.

The kingdom splits (chapters 12–13). Solomon's son Rehoboam makes a catastrophic blunder, and ten of the twelve tribes break away to form the northern kingdom of Israel under Jeroboam. To keep people from traveling to Jerusalem to worship, Jeroboam sets up golden calves, an echo of the disaster at Mount Sinai. The damage is done.

What follows is a rapid downward spiral (chapters 14–16). The book tracks the rulers of both kingdoms, north and south, and the report is mostly grim. Kings come and go. Dynasties rise and fall. Assassinations pile up. Each new king of Israel seems to outdo the last in wickedness, until we arrive at the worst of them all: Ahab.

The Elijah stories (chapters 17–19) erupt into this darkness like a thunderclap. A prophet nobody has heard of walks into the throne room and announces a drought. God hides him by a brook and feeds him through ravens. A widow's flour jar never runs empty. A dead boy comes back to life. Fire falls from heaven on Mount Carmel. Rain returns after three and a half years. And then the mighty prophet collapses in exhaustion. And God meets him not in wind, earthquake, or fire, but in a gentle whisper.

The book closes with Ahab's final chapters (chapters 20–22). Wars with Syria, a stolen vineyard, an innocent man murdered by the government, and a final battle where a "random" arrow finds the one man it was always going to find. Ahab dies exactly as God's prophets said he would. The word of God, which Ahab spent his whole reign ignoring, turns out to be the only thing that matters.

A WORD BEFORE WE BEGIN

First Kings doesn't sugarcoat anything. The heroes have real flaws. The villains are genuinely dangerous. The good guys don't always win, at least not right away. A faithful man like Naboth gets framed and executed. A courageous prophet like Micaiah gets thrown in prison. The wicked queen keeps breathing long after you'd expect God to intervene.

If that bothers you, it should. It bothered the people who lived through it too. But the Bible doesn't tell us fairy tales. It tells us the truth about what happened, and it trusts us to see God at work even when the story is painful.

And God is at work all through this book. He's working when Solomon prays at the temple. He's working when the kingdom splits. He's working through ravens and widows and whispers. He's working when fire falls and when it doesn't. He's working through prophets who speak the truth even when nobody wants to hear it. He's even working through a random arrow on a battlefield.

The thread that holds 1 Kings together isn't the kings. Most of them are failures. The thread is the word of God spoken by prophets, ignored by rulers, and fulfilled every single time. That word promised David an eternal dynasty. That word warned Solomon what idolatry would cost. That word predicted the fall of every wicked king and was right without exception.

The word of God is the real king of this book. Every human king is measured against it, and every human king falls short. Which is exactly the point. First Kings will leave you looking for a better king, one whose heart never turns away, whose kingdom never splits, whose word and life are perfectly aligned.

Israel was still waiting for that king when this book ended. They'd be waiting for a long time. But he was coming.

Let's start at the beginning, with an old king on a cold throne, and two sons fighting over what comes next.

Turn the page.

1

THE OLD KING AND THE NEW

In Marvel's *Black Panther*, King T'Chaka, the ruler of Wakanda, has been killed. His son T'Challa is supposed to take the throne. Everyone expects it, the ceremony is planned, and the transition should be smooth. But then a challenger shows up. Erik Killmonger arrives with his own claim to the throne, his own supporters, and his own plan to seize power. Suddenly, what should have been a straightforward coronation becomes a fight for the future of the entire kingdom. People are forced to choose sides. Loyalties are tested. And for a terrifying moment, it looks like the wrong person might end up in charge.

That's almost exactly what happens in the opening chapters of 1 Kings. David, Israel's greatest king, is dying. His son Solomon is supposed to take the throne—God has chosen him, and David has promised it. But another son, Adonijah, decides he's not going to wait for permission. He throws himself a coronation party, gathers powerful allies, and declares himself king before anyone can stop him. What should have been an orderly transfer of power turns into a desperate scramble, with the future of God's people hanging in the balance.

First Kings opens not with triumph but with crisis. And the question hanging over everything is the one that will echo through the entire book: Who will be king? And what kind of king will he be?

AN OLD KING IN A COLD ROOM

The very first thing we learn in 1 Kings is that David is old. Not just old—feeble. The text says he "was old and advanced in years" and that "he could not get warm" no matter how many blankets they piled on him. His servants searched throughout Israel for a beautiful young woman named Abishag to care for him and keep him warm. She attended to the king, but the text adds a pointed detail: "the king knew her not."

That might seem like a strange way to start a book. But the writer is making an important point. This is not the David you've been reading about. This is not the shepherd boy who killed Goliath. Not the warrior who danced before the ark of God. Not the king who built Jerusalem into a capital city. That David was bold, decisive, and full of energy. This David can't even keep himself warm.

The giant-slayer is now an old man in a cold room, and the whole court knows it. The king who once led armies can barely get himself out of bed. And when a king grows weak, ambitious people start to circle.

THE PRINCE WHO CROWNED HIMSELF

Enter Adonijah.

Adonijah was David's fourth son, and by this point in the story, he was the oldest one still alive. His older brothers

Amnon and Absalom were both dead—Amnon murdered by Absalom, and Absalom killed during his own rebellion against David. A second brother, Kileab, had disappeared from the story entirely (probably dead). That left Adonijah as the next in line, at least by birth order.

And Adonijah looked the part. The text tells us he was "very handsome," the same kind of description given to both Saul and Absalom before him. If you've been paying attention to the story so far, that detail should make you nervous. In Israel's history, the guys who looked most like kings often turned out to be the worst ones.

Adonijah didn't just look like a king. He acted like one. He got himself chariots and horses and fifty men to run ahead of him—exactly what his brother Absalom had done before his rebellion. He threw a massive feast at a place called the Stone of Zoheleth. He invited his brothers, important officials, and two of David's most powerful allies: Joab, the commander of the army, and Abiathar, one of the chief priests.

But look at who he didn't invite: Zadok the other chief priest, Benaiah the leader of David's personal guard, Nathan the prophet, and—most importantly—his brother Solomon.

That guest list tells you everything. Adonijah wasn't just throwing a party. He was staging a coup. He was crowning himself king while his father lay helpless in bed, hoping that by the time anyone noticed, it would be too late to stop him.

And here's the detail that explains how it got this far: "His father had never at any time displeased him by asking, 'Why have you done thus and so?'" David—the brilliant warrior, the gifted poet, the man after God's own heart—had never once told Adonijah no. He hadn't corrected him. Hadn't confronted him. Hadn't parented him.

The same failure that allowed Absalom to spiral out of control was now playing out again with another son. David's inability to deal with his boys was one of the defining weaknesses of his life, and even on his deathbed, it was still causing chaos.

THE PROPHET AND THE QUEEN

Fortunately, not everyone was asleep at the wheel. Nathan the prophet—the same Nathan who had confronted David about Bathsheba and Uriah years earlier—heard what Adonijah was doing and immediately went to work. He went to Bathsheba, Solomon's mother, with an urgent message: "Have you not heard that Adonijah has become king, and David our lord does not know it?"

Nathan wasn't just delivering news. He was sounding an alarm. If Adonijah secured the throne, Solomon and Bathsheba would both be in mortal danger. Rival claimants to ancient thrones didn't get to retire peacefully. They got killed.

So Nathan devised a plan. Bathsheba would go to David first and remind him of his oath before God that Solomon would be king after him. Then, while she was still speaking, Nathan would come in and confirm everything she said. Two witnesses. One message. A double appeal designed to cut through the fog of David's old age and force him to act.

Bathsheba went in and found David in his room, with Abishag attending to him. She bowed before the king and laid it out plainly: "My lord, you swore to me by the LORD your God: 'Solomon your son shall reign after me, and he shall sit on my throne.' But now Adonijah has become king, and you, my lord the king, do not know about it." She named names. She described the feast. She pointed out that Solomon had been excluded. And she delivered the gut punch: "The eyes of all Israel are on you, to learn from you who will sit on the throne after you. Otherwise, when you are laid to rest, I and my son Solomon will be treated as criminals."

While she was still speaking, Nathan arrived, right on cue. He added his own version of the report, carefully framing it to provoke David: "Have you, my lord the king, declared that Adonijah shall be king after you? Because that's exactly what's happening right now. And nobody told me." The strategy worked. Suddenly, the old king stirred. The David of old—decisive, bold, commanding—flickered back to life.

A KING ON A MULE

David called Bathsheba back into the room. He swore an oath: "As surely as the LORD lives, who has delivered me out of every trouble, I will surely carry out today what I swore to you by the LORD, the God of Israel: Solomon your son shall be king after me, and he will sit on my throne in my place."

Then David started giving orders—fast, specific, and sharp. "Take Solomon and set him on my own mule. Bring him down to the spring of Gihon. Have Zadok the priest and Nathan the prophet anoint him king over Israel. Blow the trumpet and shout, 'Long live King Solomon!' Then bring him back, and he will sit on my throne."

Every detail mattered. The mule was David's personal animal—riding it was a public statement that Solomon was David's chosen heir. The anointing was performed with oil from the sacred tent, connecting Solomon's kingship to God's presence. The trumpet blast and the public ceremony made it official in a way that Adonijah's private dinner party could never be.

And the people responded. When Solomon was anointed at Gihon, the celebration was so loud that "the earth was split by their noise." This wasn't a backroom deal. It was a national moment. The ground itself seemed to shake with the weight of what was happening.

THE PARTY'S OVER

Meanwhile, back at Adonijah's feast, the guests were finishing their meal when they heard the noise echoing through the valley. Joab, the seasoned military commander, heard the trumpet and asked, "What's the meaning of all the noise in the city?"

Before anyone could answer, Jonathan the son of Abiathar arrived with the news. Adonijah greeted him warmly: "Come in. A worthy man like you must be bringing good news."

Jonathan's answer was blunt: "Not at all. Our lord King David has made Solomon king." He described the whole ceremony—the mule, the anointing, the trumpet, the celebration, the fact that Solomon was already sitting on the royal throne. And then the detail that sealed it: David himself had bowed on his bed and blessed God for letting him see a successor on his throne.

The party evaporated. Every one of Adonijah's guests "rose in alarm and dispersed." Nobody wanted to be caught at the table of the losing side. Adonijah, terrified, ran to the altar of the Lord and grabbed hold of its horns—the ancient equivalent of claiming sanctuary. He begged for his life.

Solomon's response was measured but firm: "If he shows himself to be a worthy man, not a hair of his head will fall to the ground. But if evil is found in him, he will die." Adonijah was sent home. For now, he was alive. But the warning hung over him like a storm cloud.

THE LAST WORDS OF A KING

David knew his time was short. He called Solomon to his bedside and gave him one final charge. It's one of the most important speeches in the Old Testament, and it has two very different parts.

The first part is pure gold. David told Solomon to be strong and to walk in God's ways—to keep his commands, his laws, and his requirements "as written in the Law of Moses, so that you may prosper in all you do and wherever you go." He reminded Solomon of God's promise to the house of David: that there would always be a descendant on the throne, if they remained faithful.

This is David at his best: pointing his son toward God, reminding him that obedience is the foundation of everything. It doesn't matter how smart you are or how powerful your army is. If you don't walk with God, none of it will last.

But the second part of David's charge was different. David gave Solomon a list of people to deal with. Joab, who had murdered two innocent men and had just sided with Adonijah. Shimei, who had cursed David during Absalom's rebellion. And Barzillai's family, who had shown David kindness when he was on the run. David told Solomon to reward the loyal and to deal wisely with the dangerous.

Then David died. He "slept with his fathers and was buried in the city of David." After decades of war, worship, failure, and faith, the shepherd-king was gone.

ESTABLISHING THE KINGDOM

Solomon was now king, but the kingdom wasn't yet secure. Threats remained, and they surfaced quickly.

Adonijah made a fatal mistake. He went to Bathsheba (now the queen mother) and asked her to persuade Solomon to give him Abishag, the woman who had cared for David, as his wife. It might sound harmless, but in the ancient world, taking a king's companion was a way of claiming the king's authority. Whether Adonijah meant it that way or not, Solomon saw it as another grab for power.

"Why do you ask Abishag for Adonijah?" Solomon said to his mother. "You might as well ask for the kingdom for him." That same day, Solomon had Adonijah executed.

Abiathar the priest, who had supported Adonijah, was removed from his position and banished to his hometown. Solomon spared his life because of his long service to David, but his days as priest were over. This fulfilled a prophecy God had made generations earlier against the house of Eli—that his descendants would be removed from the priesthood.

Joab heard what had happened and knew he was next. He fled to the tabernacle and grabbed the horns of the altar, just as Adonijah had done before. But this time, sanctuary didn't save him. Solomon sent Benaiah to execute him. Joab had shed innocent blood throughout his career, and now that blood was answered.

Finally, there was Shimei. Solomon placed him under a kind of house arrest in Jerusalem, telling him plainly: stay in the city and live; leave, and die. For three years, Shimei obeyed. Then two of his slaves ran away to the Philistine city of Gath, and Shimei went after them. When Solomon found out, he summoned Shimei and carried out the sentence.

The narrator closes the chapter with a simple but loaded statement: "The kingdom was established in the hand of Solomon."

WHAT THIS MEANS FOR US

First, transitions can be dangerous. Every time leadership changes—in a nation, a church, a family, or even a friend group—there's a moment of vulnerability. People jockey for position. Old conflicts resurface. The kingdom of God has always passed through precarious moments, and it always will. But *God is faithful through every one of them.*

Second, passive leadership causes real damage. David's failure to discipline Adonijah—his refusal to ever say no—nearly cost Solomon the throne and could have thrown Israel into civil war. When the people in charge refuse to address problems, the problems don't go away. They grow.

Third, obedience is the foundation of everything. David's best advice to Solomon wasn't political strategy. It was simple: walk with God. Keep his commands. That's what secures a kingdom, a life, a future. Not cleverness. Not military power. Faithfulness.

Fourth, God keeps his promises even through messy situations. The politics in these chapters are complicated. The motives are mixed. The methods are sometimes brutal. But through it all, God was keeping his word to David—placing Solomon on the throne, continuing the line that would eventually lead to Jesus. God doesn't need perfect people to accomplish his purposes. He works through flawed, complicated, sometimes ruthless human beings to bring about his plan.

Fifth, how you handle power reveals your heart. Adonijah grabbed for power. Solomon received it. That difference matters. The rest of 1 Kings will show us what Solomon did with the power he was given, and whether he followed his father's dying advice.

TALKING POINTS

1. **David's inability to discipline his sons led to crisis after crisis.** Why is it important for parents (and other authority figures) to set boundaries, even when it's uncomfortable?
2. **Nathan and Bathsheba worked together to remind David of his promise.** What does their example teach us about speaking up when something important is at stake?
3. **Solomon showed Adonijah mercy at first, but when Adonijah pushed his luck, that mercy ran out.** How do you balance giving people second chances with protecting yourself and others from harm?
4. **David's final advice to Solomon had two parts: walk with God, and deal with your enemies.** Do you think those two things can go together? Why or why not?
5. **The narrator says "the kingdom was established in the hand of Solomon."** What do you think it means for a kingdom or a life to be truly "established"?

David is gone. Solomon sits on the throne. The kingdom is secure—for now. But a kingdom built on a promise is only as strong as the king's faithfulness to the one who made that promise. Solomon has the crown. He has the power. He has the throne his father fought for and the God his father trusted. The question is: what will he do with it?

Turn the page.

2

THE ONE THING SOLOMON ASKED FOR

In *Aladdin*, there's a moment every kid remembers. Aladdin is standing in the Cave of Wonders, holding a dusty old lamp that turns out to contain an all-powerful genie. The Genie bursts out in a cloud of blue smoke, stretches, cracks his knuckles, and makes the offer of a lifetime: three wishes. Anything you want. Riches? Fame? Power? You name it, you got it. The only limits are no wishing for more wishes, no making people fall in love, and no bringing anyone back from the dead. Other than that? The world is yours.

Now imagine you're Aladdin. What do you wish for?

Be honest. Most of us would go straight for the obvious stuff. Money. Popularity. A mansion. The ability to fly. Maybe unlimited pizza. Your answer to that question reveals a lot about what matters most to you.

In 1 Kings 3, God makes Solomon an offer that makes the Genie's deal look small. No three-wish limit. No fine print. Just a wide-open invitation from the Creator of the universe: "Ask what I should give you."

What Solomon asked for—and what he didn't ask for—is

one of the most famous moments in the entire Bible. And it set the stage for the most extraordinary period in Israel's history.

A LOVE THAT WASN'T PERFECT

Before we get to Solomon's request, the text drops a few details we shouldn't skip past.

First, we learn that Solomon married the daughter of Pharaoh, the king of Egypt. On one hand, this was a sign of Israel's growing importance—Egypt was the superpower of the ancient world, and Pharaoh doesn't marry his daughter to just anybody. On the other hand, the name "Egypt" carried heavy baggage for Israel. This was the nation that had enslaved their ancestors for four hundred years. God had rescued Israel from Egypt, and now Solomon was linking himself back to it through marriage. It's an early warning sign—a small crack that will eventually become a canyon.

Second, the text tells us something important about Solomon's heart: "Solomon loved the LORD, walking in the statutes of David his father." That's a genuinely positive statement. Solomon wasn't faking it. He loved God. He worshiped God. He offered sacrifices at the most important worship site in the land, the great high place at Gibeon, where the old tabernacle from Moses's day still stood.

But his love came with a qualification. He was worshiping at the high places (local shrines scattered across the countryside) because there was no temple yet. The text doesn't condemn Solomon for this, but it does make you wonder: was Solomon's love for God as wholehearted as it could have been? Was he already a little divided?

Keep that question in your back pocket. It's going to matter a lot later.

THE DREAM AT GIBEON

Solomon went to Gibeon and offered a thousand burnt offerings on the altar there. That night, God appeared to him in a dream and said five words that changed everything: "Ask what I should give you."

Think about that. The God who made the stars and the oceans and the mountains looked at this young king and essentially said, "Name it. Whatever you want, it's yours."

Solomon could have asked for anything. A long life. Endless wealth. Victory over every enemy. The kind of power that would make every other nation tremble. Any of those would have been perfectly understandable requests for a king surrounded by threats and responsibilities. But Solomon didn't ask for any of those things.

Instead, he prayed one of the most remarkable prayers in the Bible. He started by remembering what God had done for his father David, how God had shown "great and steadfast love" to David and had kept his promise by placing Solomon on the throne. Then he admitted his own weakness: "I am only a little child. I do not know how to go out or come in." He wasn't literally a child, but he felt like one. The job was enormous, and he knew he wasn't up to it on his own.

And then came the request: "Give your servant a hearing heart to judge your people, to discern between good and evil. For who is able to judge this great people of yours?" A hearing heart. Not a clever mind. Not a ruthless edge. A heart that could listen to people, to truth, to God himself, and make decisions that were wise and just. Solomon's deepest concern wasn't his own comfort or power. It was the welfare of the people God had placed in his care.

God was pleased. The text says it plainly: "It pleased the Lord that Solomon had asked this."

And then God did something extraordinary. He gave Solomon what he asked for: a wise and discerning heart, unlike anyone who had ever lived before or would ever live after. But he also gave Solomon what he hadn't asked for: riches and honor so great that no other king in his lifetime would compare to him. It's as if God said, "Because you asked for the right thing, I'm going to throw in everything else too."

There was one condition, though. God added: "If you walk in my ways, keeping my statutes and my commandments, as your father David walked, then I will lengthen your days."

If. That little word carries the weight of the world. God's gifts were real. God's promises were generous. But they came with a call to faithfulness. Solomon's future depended not just on what he received but on what he did with it.

When Solomon woke up, he returned to Jerusalem and stood before the ark of the covenant—the symbol of God's presence—and offered sacrifices and held a feast for all his servants. Something had shifted. The king who had been operating on human cleverness in chapter 2 now had something deeper. He had wisdom from God.

But would he keep it?

THE CASE OF THE TWO MOTHERS

The proof came quickly. Two women came before Solomon with a case that seemed impossible to solve. They were both living in the same house. Both had given birth within three days of each other. One night, one woman's baby died. She claimed the other woman had switched the babies in the dark, taking the living child and leaving the dead one in its place. The other woman denied it completely.

No witnesses. No evidence. No DNA tests. Just two women, one living baby, and two completely opposite stories. It was the kind of case that would stump any judge, because there was absolutely no way to determine who was telling the truth.

Solomon listened. Then he gave an order that shocked everyone in the room: "Bring me a sword."

A sword was brought. Solomon said, "Divide the living child in two, and give half to one and half to the other."

The room must have gone silent. Was the king serious? Would he actually do it?

One woman immediately cried out: "Oh, my lord, give her the living child, and by no means put him to death!" She would rather lose her son to another woman than see him killed. Her love was greater than her need to win.

The other woman said, "He shall be neither mine nor yours; divide him."

Solomon had his answer. The real mother was the one willing to give up her child to save his life. He ordered the baby given to her.

When word of this judgment spread through Israel, the people were awestruck. The text says they "feared the king, for they saw that the wisdom of God was in him to do justice." This wasn't just a clever trick. It was something deeper, a God-given ability to see through the surface of things and get to the truth.

And notice what Solomon used his new wisdom for. Not to enrich himself. Not to destroy his enemies. He used it to protect the helpless—a baby who couldn't speak for himself and a mother who had no other advocate. That's what godly wisdom looks like. It serves the people who need it most.

THE GOLDEN AGE

Chapter 4 pulls back the camera and shows us what Solomon's kingdom looked like at its peak. And the picture is stunning.

Solomon organized his government with impressive efficiency. He appointed cabinet officials to handle different areas of responsibility: a chief priest, secretaries, a military commander, a palace manager, and twelve district officers spread across the entire nation. Each district was responsible for supplying food to the royal court for one month out of the year. It was a system designed to spread the burden evenly so that no single region was crushed under the weight of supporting the king.

This might sound like boring administrative stuff, but it's actually another expression of wisdom. Godly wisdom doesn't just show up in dramatic courtroom moments. It also shows up in the quiet, unglamorous work of organizing life so that things run well and people are cared for. Good leadership isn't just about making great speeches. It's about building systems that work.

And the results spoke for themselves. The writer describes Solomon's kingdom in language that practically glows with joy: "Judah and Israel were as numerous as the sand on the seashore. They were eating and drinking and rejoicing." If you know your Old Testament, those words should jump off the page. "As numerous as the sand on the seashore"—that's the promise God made to Abraham a thousand years earlier. God had told Abraham that his descendants would be too many to count, and now, under Solomon, it had finally happened. The ancient promise was being fulfilled right before their eyes.

And it wasn't just about numbers. Solomon's kingdom extended "from the Euphrates River to the land of the Philistines, as far as the border of Egypt." Every surrounding kingdom paid tribute to Solomon. The borders were secure. The enemies were quiet. For the first time in Israel's history, the people experienced what the text calls true peace: "Judah and Israel lived in safety, each man under his vine and under his fig tree, from Dan to Beersheba, all the days of Solomon."

Each man under his vine and fig tree. That's a picture of ordinary people living without fear—growing their food, raising their families, enjoying the fruit of their labor without worrying that an army is going to show up and destroy everything. It's a vision of the world as God intended it to be.

This was the golden age. The fulfillment of centuries of promises. God had told Abraham he would make a great nation, and here it was. God had told David his son would reign in peace, and here it was. Everything God had said was coming true.

THE WISEST MAN ALIVE

The chapter closes with a celebration of Solomon's wisdom that borders on breathless. God gave Solomon "wisdom and understanding beyond measure, and breadth of mind like the sand on the seashore." His wisdom surpassed the wisdom of everyone in the ancient world: the famous sages of the East, the scholars of Egypt, and the legendary wise men whose names were known across the region.

Solomon composed three thousand proverbs and over a thousand songs. He studied and spoke about the natural world—trees, from the towering cedars of Lebanon to the tiny hyssop plants growing out of cracks in walls. He studied animals, birds, reptiles, and fish. His curiosity was boundless. His mind ranged across every subject, from morality to music to marine biology.

And people noticed. Kings and scholars came from all over the world to hear Solomon's wisdom. Israel, the little nation that had been enslaved in Egypt and nearly destroyed during the time of the judges, was now the intellectual center of the ancient world. Nations that had never heard of Israel were sending delegations just to listen to the king talk.

It was extraordinary. It was everything God had promised and more.

But there's a shadow in the text that most readers miss. Tucked into the description of Solomon's greatness is a note about his horses—forty thousand stalls for chariot horses and twelve thousand horsemen. If you remember Deuteronomy, God had specifically warned Israel's future kings not to "acquire great numbers of horses" (Deuteronomy 17:16). Horses meant military power. Military power meant trusting in your own strength instead of trusting God. It meant becoming like the nations around you instead of remaining different.

Solomon was accumulating horses. Not yet in catastrophic

numbers, but the pattern was starting. The seeds of trouble were being planted even in the middle of the golden age.

That's one of the most important lessons in the entire book of 1 Kings: danger doesn't always announce itself with a trumpet blast. Sometimes it creeps in quietly, disguised as success.

WHAT THIS MEANS FOR US

First, what you ask for reveals who you are. God's offer to Solomon was also a test. Solomon could have asked for anything, and his choice to ask for wisdom to serve God's people (instead of wealth or power or revenge) revealed the condition of his heart. The same is true for us. What we want most says more about us than what we say or even what we do.

Second, God is wildly generous. Solomon asked for one thing, and God gave him everything. Jesus said the same thing centuries later: "Seek first the kingdom of God and his righteousness, and all these things will be added to you" (Matthew 6:33). When we put God's priorities first, he takes care of the rest. Not always in the way we expect, but always in the way we need.

Third, wisdom isn't just for dramatic moments. Solomon's wisdom showed up in a courtroom, yes, but it also showed up in administrative lists and government organization and economic policy. Wisdom is for every part of life, including the parts that seem boring. How you organize your time, how you treat your responsibilities, how you manage what you've been given—that's wisdom in action.

Fourth, fulfilled promises should produce joy. The writer of 1 Kings is practically giddy describing Solomon's kingdom, because he recognizes that God is keeping promises made to Abraham and David centuries earlier. When we see God being faithful—in Scripture, in history, in our own lives—the right response is joy. God keeps his word. That should make us happy.

Fifth, watch for the seeds. Even in Solomon's golden age, warning signs were already present: the Egyptian marriage, the high places, and the accumulating horses. Sin rarely arrives all at once. It grows slowly, planted in the soil of success, watered by the assumption that the rules don't quite apply to you. If it can happen to the wisest man who ever lived, it can happen to anyone.

TALKING POINTS

1. **Solomon could have asked for wealth, power, long life, or revenge on his enemies. Instead, he asked for the ability to tell right from wrong.** If God appeared to you tonight and said, "Ask for anything you want," what would you ask for? What does your answer reveal about what matters most to you?

2. **Solomon admitted to God, "I am only a little child. I do not know how to go out or come in."** Why is admitting weakness actually a sign of wisdom? Why is it so hard to do?

3. **In the case of the two mothers, Solomon used his wisdom to protect someone who couldn't protect himself.** How can wisdom be used to serve others today—especially people who don't have power or a voice?

4. **The writer describes Solomon's kingdom as a place where "each man sat under his vine and fig tree" in safety.** What would that kind of peace look like in your neighborhood, your school, or your family?

5. **Even during the golden age, warning signs were already appearing in Solomon's life.** What are some "small" compromises that people your age face that might not seem like a big deal but could lead to bigger problems?

Solomon asked for wisdom, and God gave him the world. Under his rule, Israel became everything God had promised: a great nation, secure in its borders, overflowing with abundance, and the envy of every kingdom on earth. For one shining moment, it looked like the story had reached its happy ending.

But 1 Kings isn't a fairy tale. And happy endings that depend on human faithfulness have a way of unraveling. Solomon has the wisdom. The question is whether he'll keep listening to the God who gave it to him.

The answer is coming. Turn the page.

3

THE HOUSE WHERE GOD MOVED IN

If you've ever played Minecraft in survival mode, you know the difference between your first night and your hundredth. On night one, you're punching trees and digging a hole in the side of a hill, hoping nothing spawns nearby. You eat whatever you can find and wait for sunrise in a dirt box.

But over time (maybe weeks of real-world playing), everything changes. You mine better materials. You plan designs. You smelt glass and craft banners and figure out how to use redstone. Eventually you step back and look at what you've built—a castle, a cathedral, a fortress with towers and stained-glass windows and rooms for every purpose—and something hits you. You started with nothing, and now this exists. Every block was placed with intention. Every hallway means something because you remember when all you had was a dirt hole and a wooden pickaxe.

That satisfaction of building something magnificent after starting with nothing is a shadow of what Israel experienced in 1 Kings 5–8. For nearly five hundred years, God's people had been on the move. Slaves in Egypt. Wanderers in the desert.

Fighters in Canaan. Survivors during the judges. They worshiped God in a tent—a portable tabernacle they carried from camp to camp. It was sacred, but it was temporary. It said, "We're not home yet."

Now, under Solomon, they were finally home. The enemies were defeated. The land was secure. And for the first time in Israel's history, someone was going to build God a permanent house—not a tent, not a temporary shelter, but a temple so beautiful it would take your breath away.

But here's what makes this story more than a construction project: this house came with a condition. Its future didn't depend on the quality of the stone or the thickness of the gold. It depended on whether the king who built it would keep listening to the God who lived inside it.

And that changes everything about how we read this story.

A DREAM 480 YEARS IN THE MAKING

Before a single stone was cut, the writer drops a date that tells us something enormous: "In the four hundred and eightieth year after the Israelites had come out of Egypt, in the fourth year of Solomon's reign, he began to build the temple of the LORD."

Four hundred and eighty years. That's the distance between the exodus and this moment. Think about what happened in those centuries. Israel escaped slavery, wandered in the wilderness for forty years, conquered the promised land under Joshua, nearly destroyed themselves during the time of the judges, and finally established a monarchy under Saul and David. For nearly five centuries, God's people had been on the move—unsettled, unstable, always fighting, always wandering.

Now, finally, it was over. God had promised Abraham a land. He had promised David rest from enemies. He had promised that David's son would build a house for his name. And here it was, all of it coming true at once.

The temple wasn't just a building project. It was the finish line of a promise that had been running for almost half a millennium. The exodus wasn't just about getting Israel out of Egypt. It was about getting Israel home. And the temple was the sign that they had finally arrived.

CEDAR, STONE, AND A DEAL WITH TYRE

Solomon couldn't build the temple alone. Israel had plenty of stone, but they didn't have the right timber. For that, Solomon needed the famous cedars of Lebanon. They were massive, fragrant trees that were considered the finest building material in the ancient world.

So he made a deal with Hiram, king of Tyre, a coastal city in what we'd call Lebanon today. Hiram had been friendly with David, and he was happy to extend that relationship to David's son. When Hiram heard Solomon's plan, he praised God for giving David "a wise son over this great people."

The arrangement was simple: Hiram's skilled lumberjacks would cut the cedars and float them down the coast in rafts. Solomon would pay Hiram with massive quantities of wheat and olive oil to feed his royal court: twenty thousand cors of wheat and twenty thousand baths of oil, year after year. It was a trade deal that benefited both kingdoms.

But it was also more than a business transaction. Here was a foreign king praising the God of Israel and contributing to the construction of God's house. The cedars of Lebanon would form the walls and ceiling of the place where God chose to dwell. The nations were already being drawn into Israel's story, even if they didn't fully realize it.

Solomon assembled an enormous labor force. Thirty thousand men rotated in shifts to Lebanon—one month working, two months at home. Another seventy thousand served as carriers and eighty thousand as stonecutters in the hills. Over thirty-three hundred foremen supervised the work. The foundation stones alone were massive blocks of the finest quality, carefully dressed at the quarry so that no hammer or chisel was heard at the temple site itself. The construction was both enormous in scale and remarkably quiet, a building rising in silence, stone by stone.

A HOUSE OF GOLD

The temple itself was not large by modern standards. It was about ninety feet long, thirty feet wide, and forty-five feet tall. You could fit it inside a decent-sized gymnasium. But what it lacked in size it made up for in splendor.

The building had three main sections. First, a porch or entrance hall at the front. Then the main hall, a large room paneled entirely with cedar wood carved with gourds, open flowers, palm trees, and cherubim. The carvings turned the interior walls into an image of a garden—Eden re-created in wood and stone. And at the very back, behind carved olive-wood doors, was the inner sanctuary: the Most Holy Place. This was a perfect cube—twenty cubits long, twenty wide, twenty high—where the ark of the covenant would rest beneath the wings of two enormous golden cherubim, each fifteen feet tall, their wings stretching from wall to wall.

And then there was the gold. The writer can barely contain himself. The inner sanctuary was overlaid with pure gold. The main hall was covered with gold. The altar was gold. The floor was gold. The cherubim were gold. The doors were gold. Gold chains stretched across the entrance to the Most Holy Place. The word "gold" appears over and over like a drumbeat. The writer isn't embarrassed by this; he's amazed by it. Every surface gleamed because nothing cheap was considered worthy of the God who lived there.

Outside, a master craftsman named Huram from Tyre cast two enormous bronze pillars for the entrance, each twenty-seven feet tall, topped with elaborate capitals decorated with pomegranates and lily designs. One pillar was named Jakin, meaning "he establishes," and the other Boaz, meaning "in him is strength." Every time a priest walked between those pillars to enter the temple, he passed between two reminders: God establishes, and God is strong. You don't come into this place on your own power.

Huram also cast a massive bronze basin called "the Sea"—fifteen feet across, seven and a half feet deep, resting on the backs of twelve bronze bulls facing outward in groups of three toward the four compass points. It held about eleven thousand gallons of water. Ten smaller basins on wheeled bronze stands were placed along the sides of the temple, each one elaborately decorated with lions, bulls, cherubim, and palm trees.

The writer spends an astonishing amount of space describing all this detail—every measurement, every decoration, every material. Why? Because he believes that careful, beautiful craftsmanship honors God. Nothing was thrown together. Nothing was "good enough." Everything was done with the kind of attention that says, "The one who lives here deserves our very best."

THE INTERRUPTION THAT MATTERS MOST

Right in the middle of the construction report, between the description of the exterior and the interior, the writer drops something unexpected. God speaks directly to Solomon:

"As for this temple you are building—if you follow my decrees, carry out my regulations and keep all my commands and obey them, I will fulfill through you the promise I gave to David your father. And I will live among the Israelites and will not abandon my people Israel."

God interrupts a construction report. Why? Because there's something more important than walls and gold and cedar panels. The temple is beautiful, but beauty without obedience is an empty shell. God isn't impressed by architecture. He's looking for faithfulness. The promise is real—"I will live among the Israelites"—but it comes with a condition: "if you follow my decrees." The temple's future depends on Solomon's heart, not Solomon's budget.

This interruption signals priorities. It's as if God is saying, "I see the building going up, and it's wonderful. But don't lose sight of what really matters. This house is nothing without the relationship."

THE DAY THE CLOUD MOVED IN

Seven years after the first stone was laid, the temple was finished. And now came the moment everyone had been waiting for.

Solomon assembled all the leaders of Israel in Jerusalem during the Festival of Tabernacles—the great harvest celebration that recalled Israel's wilderness wandering. The timing was perfect. The festival that remembered homelessness became the occasion for God to come home.

The priests carried the ark of the covenant into the inner sanctuary and set it beneath the wings of the golden cherubim. The text pauses to note something remarkable: "There was nothing in the ark except the two stone tablets that Moses had placed in it at Horeb." The ark didn't contain treasure or weapons. It contained God's words, the Ten Commandments. The heart of the temple was the word of God.

And then it happened.

When the priests came out of the Holy Place, "the cloud filled the temple of the LORD, and the priests could not perform their service because of the cloud, for the glory of the LORD filled his temple."

God showed up. Not in a vision. Not in a dream. In a visible, overwhelming, room-filling cloud of glory so powerful that the priests had to stop what they were doing and back away. This was the same glory-cloud that had led Israel through the wilderness, the same cloud that had filled the tabernacle when Moses finished it centuries earlier. Now it filled this permanent house. God was home.

Solomon's response captured the awe of the moment: "The LORD has said that he would dwell in a thick cloud. I have indeed built a magnificent temple for you, a place for you to dwell forever."

THE GREATEST PRAYER IN THE OLD TESTAMENT

Then Solomon knelt before the altar, spread his hands toward heaven, and prayed what may be the most remarkable prayer in the entire Old Testament.

He started with praise: "LORD, the God of Israel, there is no God like you in heaven above or on earth below—you who keep your covenant of love." God is incomparable. There is no one else like him. And the proof? He keeps his promises. What he said to David, he has done. "You spoke with your mouth and with your hand you have fulfilled it."

Then Solomon said something stunning for a king standing in front of his greatest achievement: "But will God really dwell on earth? The heavens, even the highest heaven, cannot contain you. How much less this temple I have built!"

In other words: I know this building can't hold you. The universe can't hold you. You are bigger than anything we could ever construct. And yet—and this is the miracle—you have chosen to be here. You have chosen to make yourself available. You have chosen to listen.

The rest of Solomon's prayer is built around one repeated word: hear. Hear from heaven. Hear our prayers. Hear when we sin and repent. Hear when disaster strikes. Solomon walks through seven different scenarios—situations where Israel would desperately need God's attention. What happens when someone wrongs their neighbor and takes an oath at the altar? Hear. When Israel is defeated by an enemy because of sin? Hear and forgive. When there's no rain? When famine or plague strikes? When a foreigner comes to pray? When the army goes to battle? When—and Solomon says "when," not "if"—the people sin so badly that they are carried into exile?

Even then, Solomon prays, if they turn back to you with all their heart, hear from heaven and forgive.

Solomon's prayer holds two truths in tension. On one hand, God is so vast that the universe can't contain him. On the other, God is so close that he bends down to hear the whispered prayer of a single person. He is both immense and intimate. Too big for heaven, yet willing to listen from a temple in Jerusalem. That combination—a God who is beyond everything yet available to everyone—is one of the most beautiful ideas in the Bible.

And notice who Solomon included in his prayer: the foreigner. The outsider who doesn't belong to Israel but has heard about this God and comes to pray. Solomon asked God to hear that person's prayer too, "so that all the peoples of the earth may know your name." From the very beginning, the temple was supposed to be more than Israel's private chapel. It was meant to be a light to the world.

THE PARTY

When the prayer ended, the celebration began. Solomon offered twenty-two thousand cattle and one hundred and twenty thousand sheep. The numbers are staggering—this was a feast that fed the entire nation. The bronze altar in the courtyard wasn't big enough, so Solomon consecrated the entire middle of the courtyard for offerings. For seven days the people celebrated, and then for seven more. Fourteen days of feasting, worship, and joy.

When the people finally went home, they went "joyful and glad in heart for all the good things the LORD had done." The word the text uses for going home is actually "to their tents"—the same word that had described Israel's wandering existence for centuries. They were going to their tents, but now they had a temple. The wandering was over.

It was the high point of Israel's entire history. Everything God had promised had come true. The people were many. The land was secure. The king was wise. The temple was built. God's glory filled the house.

WHAT THIS MEANS FOR US

First, God finishes what he starts. Four hundred and eighty years separated the exodus from the temple. That's an almost incomprehensible amount of time. But God wasn't in a hurry, and he didn't forget. He made a promise to Abraham, renewed it to Moses, confirmed it to David, and fulfilled it through Solomon. If God takes a long time to complete something in your life, it doesn't mean he's abandoned the project.

Second, beauty matters to God. The detailed descriptions of gold and cedar and bronze aren't filler—they're worship. The writer believes that careful, excellent, beautiful work honors the God who made a beautiful world. Whether it's a school project, a piece of art, a meal you cook, or the way you treat your room—doing things with care and excellence is a form of honoring the one who made you.

Third, God is bigger than any box we build for him. Solomon's prayer is a masterclass in holding two truths at once: God is uncontainably vast, yet incredibly close. No building, no tradition, no system can capture all of who God is. And yet he chooses to be near. He listens. He forgives. That combination of majesty and tenderness is what makes him unlike any other.

Fourth, faithfulness matters more than architecture. God interrupted the building project to remind Solomon that obedience matters more than gold-plated walls. A beautiful church, a perfect Sunday, a flawless worship service—none of it means anything without a heart that listens to God. The building is nothing without the relationship.

Fifth, the temple was always meant for everyone. Solomon's prayer for the foreigner reminds us that God's house was never supposed to be an exclusive club. From the very beginning, God intended his presence to be a magnet that drew all kinds of people from all kinds of places.

TALKING POINTS

1. **The temple took seven years to build.** What's something in your life that required patience and long-term effort? How does it feel when you finally see it completed?

2. **God interrupted the construction to remind Solomon about obedience.** Why do you think God cared more about Solomon's heart than the building's beauty?

3. **Solomon said even the highest heavens couldn't contain God—yet God chose to dwell in a temple.** What does that tell you about the kind of God he is?

4. **Solomon's prayer covered all kinds of situations—defeat, drought, plague, exile.** Why do you think he included so many worst-case scenarios in a prayer that was supposed to be a celebration?

5. **Solomon specifically prayed for foreigners who would come to the temple.** What does that tell us about who God's invitation is for?

The temple stood gleaming on its hilltop, filled with the glory of God, surrounded by a nation that had never been happier. It was the best day Israel had ever known.

But the writer who recorded all this knew something the celebrating crowds didn't. He knew how the story ended. He knew about the cracks that were coming. The house was standing. The question was whether the king would keep listening to the God who lived inside it.

Turn the page.

4

THE WISEST FOOL IN THE WORLD

In *Star Wars*, there's a character who was supposed to be the greatest of them all. Anakin Skywalker had more raw potential than any Jedi who had ever lived. He was the Chosen One—the person the ancient prophecies said would bring balance to the Force. He was gifted, powerful, brave, and mentored by the best teachers the Jedi Order had to offer. Yoda himself said, "The Chosen One, the boy may be."

And for a while, Anakin lived up to every expectation. He became a hero of the Clone Wars, a brilliant pilot, a fierce warrior. He married the woman he loved. He had everything.

But then it started to unravel. Not all at once. Slowly. Anakin's attachments became possessions. His fear of losing people turned into a willingness to do anything—even terrible things—to hold on to what he had. One compromise led to another, and by the time he knelt before Emperor Palpatine, the hero was gone. The Chosen One had become Darth Vader.

That's the shape of Solomon's story in 1 Kings 9–11. The wisest man who ever lived, blessed beyond measure by God, surrounded by gold and glory and peace—gradually, quietly, catastrophically turns away from the God who gave him everything. It may be the most heartbreaking chapter in the Old Testament.

GOD'S SECOND VISIT

After Solomon finished the temple and the royal palace—a construction project that spanned twenty years—God appeared to him a second time. The first time, at Gibeon, God had offered Solomon anything he wanted. Solomon had asked for wisdom, and God had given him the world. That first dream launched Solomon into greatness.

This second appearance was different. It wasn't an open-ended offer. It was a warning.

God began with a promise. He accepted the temple and consecrated it: "I have put my Name there forever. My eyes and my heart will always be there." The temple Solomon had built was real. God's presence in it was real. The prayers offered there would be heard.

But then came the condition: "As for you, if you walk before me faithfully with integrity of heart and uprightness, as David your father did, and do all I command, I will establish your royal throne over Israel forever."

And then the warning—sharp, detailed, and unmistakable: "But if you or your descendants turn away from me and do not observe the commands and decrees I have given you and go off to serve other gods and worship them, then I will cut Israel off from the land I have given them, and I will reject this temple I have consecrated for my Name."

God didn't leave anything to the imagination. If Solomon

turned away, the people would lose the land. The breathtaking temple covered in gold from floor to ceiling, where God's glory had fallen like a thundercloud, would become a pile of rubble. Passers-by would stare at the ruins and ask, "Why did the LORD do this?" And the answer would echo through the generations: "Because they abandoned the LORD their God."

This was not a vague threat. It was a prophecy disguised as a warning. God told Solomon exactly what would happen if he broke faith. And Solomon heard every word.

THE PEAK OF THE MOUNTAIN

Before the fall comes the summit. And what a summit it was. Chapter 10 gives us Solomon at the absolute peak of his power, and the centerpiece is the visit of the Queen of Sheba. She arrived from the southern end of the Arabian Peninsula (modern-day Yemen) with a massive caravan loaded with spices, gold, and precious stones. She had heard reports of Solomon's wisdom and wanted to test him herself.

She tested him with hard questions, riddles, and puzzles, the kind of intellectual challenges that only the sharpest minds could handle. Solomon answered every single one. "Nothing was too hard for the king to explain to her."

But it wasn't just his answers that amazed her. It was everything else: the food on his table, the organization of his officials, the way his servants were dressed, the burnt offerings he presented at the temple. When she had seen it all, the text says, "there was no more breath in her." She was literally breathless. "The report I heard in my own country about your achievements and your wisdom is true," she told him. "But I did not believe these things until I came and saw with my own eyes. Indeed, not even half was told me."

She gave Solomon 120 talents of gold (roughly four and a half tons) along with enormous quantities of spices and precious stones. Solomon gave her everything she asked for in return. Then she went home.

The writer stacks detail upon detail to make sure you feel the sheer scale of Solomon's wealth. Every year, 666 talents of gold flowed into his treasury. He made two hundred large shields of hammered gold and three hundred smaller ones. His throne was made of ivory overlaid with gold, with twelve lions standing on its six steps—unlike anything in any other kingdom. All his drinking vessels were gold. Silver was so common in Jerusalem that it was "considered as nothing."

Solomon had a fleet of trading ships that sailed to distant ports and came back every three years loaded with gold, silver, ivory, apes, and baboons. He had fourteen hundred chariots and twelve thousand horses, stationed in chariot cities across the kingdom. Kings from all over the world sought audiences with him, bringing gifts year after year.

The writer sums it up in a single line: "King Solomon was greater in riches and wisdom than all the other kings of the earth." This was the mountaintop. The highest point Israel would ever reach. Everything God promised had been fulfilled—and then some.

But mountaintops are dangerous places. Because from there, there's only one direction to go.

THE TURNING OF THE HEART

Chapter 11 opens with a sentence that lands like a hammer blow: "King Solomon loved many foreign women." The writer lists them: Moabites, Ammonites, Edomites, Sidonians, Hittites—women from the very nations God had specifically warned Israel about. "You must not intermarry with them," God had said, "because they will surely turn your hearts after their gods." It wasn't a suggestion. It was a direct command with a specific reason attached to it.

Solomon ignored it. He had seven hundred wives of royal birth and three hundred concubines. The numbers are staggering. Many of these were political marriages, alliances sealed with foreign powers. But the text isn't interested in Solomon's diplomacy. It's interested in his heart. And the verdict is devastating: "He held fast to them in love."

Remember where this story started? "Solomon loved the LORD" (3:3). That was the opening note of his reign. Now, eight chapters later, the same verb—*loved*—has a different object. The man who loved God now clings to the very people God told him to avoid.

And then the worst sentence in the chapter: "As Solomon grew old, his wives turned his heart after other gods, and his heart was not fully devoted to the LORD his God, as the heart of David his father had been." The word "heart" appears five times in just three verses. The Bible doesn't use "heart" the way we do. It doesn't just mean feelings. It means the center of who you are: your mind, your will, your loyalties. The core of the person. And Solomon's core had shifted.

It didn't happen overnight. The text says "as Solomon grew old." This wasn't a sudden crisis. It was a slow drift that took years—decades, even—of small compromises stacking up like dust on a shelf. A marriage here. A shrine there. A worship practice tolerated. A conviction quietly set aside. One day Solomon looked up and realized he was someone he never intended to become.

He built a high place for Chemosh, the god of Moab. He built one for Molech, the god of the Ammonites, a deity associated with child sacrifice. He built shrines for all his foreign wives so they could burn incense and offer sacrifices to their gods. On the hillside east of Jerusalem, overlooking the temple he had built for the God of Israel, Solomon erected altars to the gods of the nations.

The man who built God's house built houses for God's rivals.

THE ANGER AND THE PROMISE

"The LORD became angry with Solomon." The text doesn't soften this. Twice, God had appeared to Solomon, and both times he had specifically warned him about going after other gods. Solomon had been told directly, personally, clearly. And he did it anyway.

God's anger wasn't random or petty. It was the response of a love that had been betrayed. When someone makes an exclusive promise to you and then gives their devotion to someone else, the appropriate response is anger. God's jealousy isn't insecurity; it's the character of a love that has a rightful, exclusive claim.

So God told Solomon: "Since this is your attitude and you have not kept my covenant and my decrees, I will most certainly tear the kingdom away from you and give it to one of your subordinates." But then came something unexpected. Even in judgment, God added two qualifications, two acts of mercy woven into the punishment.

First, "I will not do it during your lifetime." The full consequences would be delayed. Not because Solomon deserved the delay, but "for the sake of David your father." David, for all his failures, had never worshiped other gods. And God remembered David's faithfulness even when David's son forgot it.

Second, "I will not tear the whole kingdom away." Solomon's son would retain one tribe (Judah), again "for the sake of David my servant and for the sake of Jerusalem, which I have chosen." The kingdom would be ripped apart, but it wouldn't be annihilated. A thread of promise would remain.

Here is one of the most important principles in the entire Bible: God's judgment does not cancel God's promise. He had told David, "Your throne will be established forever." Solomon's sin was real, and the consequences were devastating, but they operated within the framework of a promise that God refused to abandon. Affliction, yes. Abandonment, no.

THE ADVERSARIES RISE

Immediately, the cracks appeared. God raised up Hadad the Edomite, a prince whose family had been destroyed by David's armies years earlier. Hadad had escaped to Egypt as a boy, grew up in Pharaoh's court, married Pharaoh's sister-in-law, and waited. When he heard David and Joab were dead, he returned to Edom and became a thorn in Solomon's side from the south.

God also raised up Rezon, a former servant of a Syrian king David had defeated. Rezon had gathered a band of rebels around him and eventually seized Damascus, the capital of Syria. He became an adversary from the north.

And then there was Jeroboam. Jeroboam was one of Solomon's own officials—a talented, hardworking young man from the tribe of Ephraim. Solomon had noticed his ability and promoted him to oversee the labor force from the northern tribes. He was exactly the kind of person a king wants in his administration: capable, energetic, a natural leader.

One day, the prophet Ahijah from Shiloh intercepted Jeroboam on a road outside Jerusalem. Ahijah was wearing a brand-new cloak, and without explanation he took it off and ripped it into twelve pieces. Then he held out ten pieces to the stunned Jeroboam and said: "Take ten pieces for yourself, for this is what the LORD, the God of Israel, says: 'I am going to tear the kingdom out of Solomon's hand and give you ten tribes.'"

It was a dramatic, unforgettable act. Prophets in the Old Testament didn't just say things. They acted them out, made them visible. A torn cloak became a torn kingdom. And the man standing there holding ten pieces of it was the future king of the northern tribes.

But even in this devastating prophecy, God made sure Jeroboam heard the grace note: "I will not take the whole kingdom out of Solomon's hand. For the sake of David my servant and for the sake of Jerusalem, I will give one tribe to his son, so that David my servant may always have a lamp before me in Jerusalem."

A lamp. Just one. But it would not go out. In the darkest moment of Solomon's story, God promised to keep a light burning. The dynasty would survive—not because Solomon deserved it, but because God's promise to David was built on something stronger than human faithfulness.

When Solomon heard what Ahijah had told Jeroboam, he tried to kill him. The wisest man in the world, the king who had once asked God for a hearing heart, now tried to murder the man God had chosen. Jeroboam fled to Egypt, to Pharaoh's protection, and waited there until Solomon died.

THE END

Solomon reigned for forty years. Then he died and was buried in Jerusalem, the City of David. His son Rehoboam succeeded him. The text gives Solomon's death exactly one verse. After nine chapters of glory, wisdom, gold, and catastrophe, the writer wraps it up in a single sentence. No eulogy. No final speech. No deathbed repentance.

The silence is deafening.

WHAT THIS MEANS FOR US

First, no gift protects you from drift. Solomon had more wisdom than any human being who ever lived. It was a supernatural gift from God himself. And yet wisdom didn't prevent Solomon from making the worst decision of his life. Knowledge of what's right doesn't automatically produce the will to do it. Faithfulness requires daily, deliberate choices, not just a one-time gift.

Second, slow drift is more dangerous than sudden disaster. Solomon's fall wasn't dramatic. Nobody woke up one morning and found the king worshiping Molech. It happened over years, through marriages, compromises, and quiet accommodations. The most dangerous sins are the ones you don't notice because they arrive one small step at a time.

Third, God keeps his promises even when we break ours. Solomon shattered his end of the covenant, and the consequences were severe. But God didn't throw out the promise he had made to David. One tribe remained. A lamp kept burning. God's faithfulness outlasted Solomon's failure. That doesn't make sin harmless; the damage was real and lasting. But it means that human failure doesn't have the final word.

Fourth, what you love determines where you end up. The heart of Solomon's problem was his heart. His affections shifted. He gave his devotion to people and things that God had told him to avoid. The Bible's most consistent warning isn't about behavior; it's about love. What you love most will shape everything else.

Fifth, even in judgment, God leaves a light on. A torn kingdom. A broken promise. A ruined legacy. But through it all, a lamp in Jerusalem. God's judgment is real, but it's not the end of the story. Even when everything falls apart, he preserves enough to rebuild from.

TALKING POINTS

1. **Anakin Skywalker fell because he was afraid of losing things he loved. Solomon fell because he loved the wrong things.** What's the difference, and what's the similarity?
2. **God warned Solomon twice.** Why do you think the warnings weren't enough to keep him faithful?

3. **The text says Solomon's drift happened "as he grew old."** Why might later seasons of life be especially dangerous for faithfulness? Can you think of ways young people might experience the same kind of slow drift?

4. **God tore the kingdom but kept one tribe for David's sake.** What does it mean that God punishes and preserves at the same time?

5. **Solomon's story begins with "Solomon loved the LORD" and ends with "Solomon loved many foreign women."** What warning does that give us about guarding our deepest affections?

Solomon started with everything. Wisdom. Wealth. Peace. A temple filled with the glory of God. A kingdom stretching from the Euphrates to Egypt. The admiration of the entire world. He ended with a torn kingdom, a death sentence on a servant, and shrines to foreign gods casting shadows across the hill from God's house.

The golden age was over. The kingdom was about to split in two. And everything that came next—every war, every wicked king, every prophet crying in the wilderness—traces back to this moment, when the wisest man alive stopped listening to the God who had given him everything.

Turn the page.

5

THE DAY EVERYTHING SPLIT

In *Captain America: Civil War*, the Avengers tear themselves apart. Not because some alien invasion forces them to, but because of a disagreement among themselves. Tony Stark wants oversight and accountability. Steve Rogers wants freedom to act. Both have a point. Both make mistakes. And by the end, the team that once saved the world together is broken in two, with former friends fighting each other in an airport parking lot.

What makes the movie so painful isn't the action. It's that you can see it coming. Every conversation that could have gone differently. Every moment where somebody could have listened instead of pushed back. And once the split happens, it can't be undone. The damage ripples forward into everything that follows.

That's 1 Kings 12. The golden kingdom of Solomon—the most powerful, prosperous, united Israel had ever been—cracks right down the middle. Not because of an invasion. Because of a conversation. A young king refuses to listen, and in a single afternoon, a nation that took centuries to build falls apart. And it never comes back together again.

THE ASSEMBLY AT SHECHEM

Solomon was dead. His son Rehoboam traveled north to Shechem to be confirmed as king over the entire nation. This wasn't a coronation in Jerusalem, surrounded by loyal supporters. Shechem was deep in northern territory—a place loaded with history. It's where Joshua had gathered all the tribes for covenant renewal after the conquest. It's where Israel's earliest leaders had met to make decisions together. Going to Shechem meant Rehoboam understood, at least in theory, that the northern tribes weren't automatically his. Their loyalty had to be earned.

And those northern tribes had a spokesperson: Jeroboam. Remember him? The talented young official Solomon had tried to kill after the prophet Ahijah tore a cloak into twelve pieces and handed him ten? Jeroboam had been hiding in Egypt ever since. Now Solomon was dead, and Jeroboam came home to lead the northern delegation.

Their demand was straightforward: "Your father put a heavy yoke on us, but now lighten the harsh labor and the heavy yoke he put on us, and we will serve you."

This was a negotiation, not a rebellion—at least not yet. The northern tribes were saying, "We're willing to follow you, but Solomon's policies were crushing us. The taxes. The forced labor. The endless building projects. Give us some relief, and we're yours."

Rehoboam asked for three days to think it over.

TWO SETS OF ADVISORS

During those three days, Rehoboam consulted two groups of people. The first were the older men who had served his father

Solomon—experienced advisors who had watched how government actually worked. Their counsel was clear and wise: "If today you will be a servant to these people and serve them and give them a favorable answer, they will always be your servants."

Did you catch that? They told the king that the way to lead is to serve. If you make yourself a servant to the people for one day, they'll be loyal to you for a lifetime. Bend a little now, and you'll have their hearts forever.

It was brilliant advice. Rehoboam ignored it.

Instead, he turned to the young men who had grown up with him—his friends, his peers, the guys who had been living in Solomon's palace their whole lives and knew nothing except privilege. These young advisors had never experienced what it was like to be an ordinary Israelite crushed under heavy taxes. They'd never carried stones or worked the labor gangs. All they knew was power, and they thought power meant intimidation.

Their advice was a masterpiece of arrogance: "Tell them, 'My little finger is thicker than my father's waist. My father laid on you a heavy yoke; I will make it even heavier. My father scourged you with whips; I will scourge you with scorpions.'"

In other words: You think Solomon was tough? You haven't seen anything yet.

THE SPLIT

On the third day, the people returned. Rehoboam stood before the assembled tribes of Israel and delivered his answer. He rejected the counsel of the experienced elders. He spoke harshly, using the exact words his young friends had crafted—the bit about whips and scorpions.

The northern tribes heard it and made their decision on the spot: "What share do we have in David? We have no inheritance in the son of Jesse. To your tents, Israel! Look after your own house, David!"

And just like that, they walked away. Ten tribes. Gone.

Rehoboam still didn't understand what had happened. He sent Adoram—the official in charge of forced labor, of all people—to go talk to the northerners. It was the worst possible choice of messenger. The northern tribes stoned Adoram to death. Only then did Rehoboam realize this was serious, and he scrambled into his chariot and fled back to Jerusalem.

Rehoboam gathered 180,000 soldiers from Judah and Benjamin to march north and force the rebels back into line. But God sent a prophet named Shemaiah with a message: "Do not go up to fight against your brothers, the Israelites. Go home, every one of you, for this is my doing."

This is my doing. That line changes everything. The writer has already told us in verse 15 that Rehoboam's stubbornness "was a turn of affairs brought about by the LORD, to fulfill the word the LORD had spoken to Jeroboam through Ahijah the Shilonite."

Rehoboam was foolish. His young advisors were reckless. The northern tribes were fed up. All of that was true. But underneath the human drama, God was keeping his word. He had told Solomon the kingdom would be torn. He had told Jeroboam through Ahijah's torn cloak that ten tribes would be his. And now, through the free decisions of real people making real choices, God's word came to pass exactly as promised.

Human stupidity is real. But it never runs loose outside of God's control.

JEROBOAM'S GOLDEN CALVES

Now Jeroboam had what he'd been promised: ten tribes and a kingdom of his own. God had even given him the same offer he once gave David—if Jeroboam walked faithfully, God would establish his dynasty forever. It was a staggering opportunity.

Jeroboam threw it away almost immediately.

His problem was practical, or so he thought. Three times a year, Israelites were supposed to travel to Jerusalem to worship at the temple. But Jerusalem was in Judah, Rehoboam's territory. Jeroboam panicked: "If these people go up to offer sacrifices at the temple of the LORD in Jerusalem, they will again give their allegiance to Rehoboam king of Judah. They will kill me and return to King Rehoboam."

Fear drove every decision that followed. Jeroboam wasn't thinking about God's promises. He was thinking about losing his grip on power. And fear made him do something breathtakingly foolish.

He made two golden calves. He set one up in Bethel, near the southern border, and one in Dan, at the far north. Then he told the people: "It is too much for you to go up to Jerusalem. Here are your gods, Israel, who brought you up out of Egypt."

Those words are almost a direct quote of what Aaron said at Mount Sinai when Moses was on the mountain and the people demanded visible gods. Jeroboam wasn't just making a political calculation. He was replaying the worst moment in Israel's history—the golden calf incident that nearly destroyed the nation before it even entered the promised land.

But he wasn't done. He built shrines on high places. He appointed priests from any tribe, not just the Levites that God had designated. He invented a festival in the eighth month to rival the Festival of Tabernacles in the seventh month. He rewrote the entire worship system of Israel from top to bottom.

The man who had started as a new Moses—leading oppressed people away from a Pharaoh-like king—had become a new Aaron, fashioning golden calves for the people to worship.

This is what fear does when it replaces faith. Jeroboam had God's own promise that his dynasty would endure if he was faithful. But instead of trusting that promise, he trusted his own political instincts. And his instincts told him that controlling people's worship was the key to controlling their loyalty.

It was the founding sin of the northern kingdom. And it would define every king who came after him. For the rest of 1 and 2 Kings, northern kings will be judged by a single standard: did they continue "the sins of Jeroboam son of Nebat, who caused Israel to sin"? That phrase becomes a drumbeat—repeated over and over and over—all the way to the destruction of the northern kingdom two hundred years later.

THE MAN OF GOD AT BETHEL

Right in the middle of Jeroboam's brand-new worship system, God interrupted. Jeroboam was standing at the altar in Bethel, about to burn incense at his counterfeit festival, when a man of God arrived from Judah. Without introduction, without permission, this unnamed prophet walked straight up to the altar and shouted a prophecy against it: "Altar, altar! This is what the LORD says: 'A son named Josiah will be born to the house of David. On you he will sacrifice the priests of the high places who make offerings here, and human bones will be burned on you.'"

This was extraordinary. The man of God named a specific person—Josiah—who wouldn't be born for another three hundred years. And he announced a sign to prove it: "This altar will be split apart and the ashes on it will be poured out."

Jeroboam's face went red. He pointed at the prophet and barked an order: "Seize him!" But the moment Jeroboam stretched out his hand, it froze. He couldn't pull it back. His arm was paralyzed. At the same instant, the altar cracked open and the ashes poured out, exactly as the man of God had predicted.

The king who had just been flexing his authority was suddenly helpless. He changed his tone in a hurry: "Intercede with the LORD your God and pray for me that my hand may be restored." Notice the pronoun—"your God," not "my God." Even in desperation, Jeroboam kept his distance from the God who had just displayed unmistakable power right in front of him.

The man of God prayed, and Jeroboam's hand was restored.

Then Jeroboam tried a different approach. "Come home with me, have something to eat, and I will give you a gift." It was a smooth diplomatic move. If the prophet would accept the king's hospitality, it would soften the sting of the public humiliation. Maybe the prophet's message could be managed.

The man of God refused flatly: "Even if you were to give me half your possessions, I would not go with you, nor would I eat bread or drink water here. For I was commanded by the word of the LORD: 'You must not eat bread or drink water or return by the way you came.'"

His refusal was an acted sermon. By refusing to eat or drink in Bethel, the man of God was treating Jeroboam's kingdom as a place cut off from fellowship with God. You don't sit down to dinner with people you've just excommunicated. The prophet's empty stomach was as much a message as his spoken words.

God gave Jeroboam a barrage of signs that day. A sign of power: the paralyzed hand. A sign of truth: the torn altar. A sign of grace: the restored hand. It was mercy—aggressive, uncomfortable, public mercy. God was giving Jeroboam every possible reason to repent and turn back.

THE LYING PROPHET

What happened next is one of the strangest and most disturbing stories in the entire Old Testament.

An old prophet who lived in Bethel heard what had happened at the altar. He saddled his donkey and chased down the man of God, finding him resting under a tree on his way home. The old prophet invited him to come back for a meal. The man of God refused, repeating his orders: no eating, no drinking, no going back.

Then the old prophet lied: "I too am a prophet, as you are. And an angel spoke to me by the word of the LORD: 'Bring him back with you to your house so that he may eat bread and drink water.'" It was a complete fabrication. The writer tells us bluntly: "He was lying to him."

And the man of God went with him. No argument. No suspicion. No questions. He simply followed the old prophet back to his house and sat down to eat.

While they were eating, a genuine word from God suddenly came to the old prophet, and it was a word of judgment against his guest. Because the man of God had disobeyed the direct command he'd received, he would not make it home alive.

After the meal, the man of God set out on a borrowed donkey. On the road, a lion met him and killed him. But then something strange happened—the lion didn't eat the body or attack the donkey. It simply stood there beside the dead man, like a sentinel. People passing by saw the bizarre scene: a corpse, a donkey, and a lion, all standing together on the road.

The old prophet retrieved the body and buried it in his own tomb, mourning over the man of God and instructing his sons: "When I die, bury me in the grave where the man of God is buried. Lay my bones beside his bones. For the message he declared by the word of the LORD against the altar in Bethel will certainly come true."

Even a lying prophet knew that God's word was reliable.

And Jeroboam? The chapter ends with a devastating one-liner: "Even after this, Jeroboam did not change his evil ways." He saw the paralyzed hand. He saw the split altar. He heard the prophecy. He watched God's word come true right before his eyes. And he went right back to appointing illegitimate priests and worshiping at his golden calves.

The word of God was his mercy. And he threw it away.

WHAT THIS MEANS FOR US

First, the people you listen to will shape your future. Rehoboam had access to wise counsel. He chose to ignore it because he preferred the advice that sounded tough and powerful. The people you surround yourself with—the voices you actually listen to—will determine the direction of your life.

Second, fear is a terrible advisor. Jeroboam had a promise from God. But fear made him think he needed to take matters into his own hands. When we make decisions out of fear rather than faith, we almost always build golden calves—substitutes for the real thing that feel safer but lead to disaster.

Third, God's word always comes true. The torn cloak became a torn kingdom. The predicted altar split exactly as announced. Three hundred years later, a king named Josiah did exactly what the man of God prophesied. God's word doesn't have an expiration date. What he says, he does.

Fourth, past faithfulness doesn't guarantee future obedience. The man of God was rock-solid against the king's pressure. He didn't flinch when Jeroboam tried intimidation. He didn't budge when offered gifts. But he collapsed when a fellow prophet told him a convincing lie. Sometimes we survive the big tests and fail the subtle ones.

Fifth, God's mercy can look like disruption. Jeroboam didn't experience the man of God's visit as mercy. It felt like embarrassment, confrontation, and threat. But God was giving him every chance to turn around. Sometimes the most loving thing God does is interrupt our plans.

TALKING POINTS

1. **Rehoboam's older advisors told him to be a servant.** Why is that advice so hard for leaders to follow? Can you think of leaders—in school, sports, or elsewhere—who lead by serving?

2. **Jeroboam was afraid the people would go back to Jerusalem if they kept worshiping there.** What was he really afraid of? How does fear lead to bad decisions in your own life?

3. **The man of God resisted the king but fell for the lying prophet.** Why do you think it's sometimes easier to stand up to obvious pressure than to handle subtle deception?

4. **After everything that happened at the altar, Jeroboam "did not change his evil ways."** What does it take for someone to actually change? Why isn't even dramatic evidence always enough?

5. **The kingdom split because of human foolishness, but the writer says it was "from the LORD."** How can something be both a human mistake and part of God's plan at the same time?

In a single chapter, Israel went from one kingdom to two. The golden age was over. The united monarchy that Saul had started, David had established, and Solomon had glorified was finished—and it would never be reassembled.

From here on, the story of 1 Kings follows two tracks: a southern kingdom called Judah, clinging to David's line and the temple in Jerusalem, and a northern kingdom called Israel, defined by Jeroboam's golden calves and counterfeit worship.

Both kingdoms were headed for trouble. But the word of God—spoken by prophets, acted out in torn cloaks and split altars, confirmed by paralyzed hands and undisturbed lions—that word would outlast every king who ignored it.

Turn the page.

6

THE LONG SLIDE DOWN

If you've read the Harry Potter books, you know about the Defense Against the Dark Arts position at Hogwarts. It's cursed. Every year, a new teacher takes the job, and every year, that teacher is gone by June. Quirrell. Lockhart. Lupin. Moody (well, the fake one). Umbridge. Some are better than others, but none of them lasts. The curse just keeps cycling through, and the position itself seems to attract trouble.

First Kings 14–16 feels like that—except the curse is real, and the stakes are life and death.

After the kingdom splits, the writer of 1 Kings takes us on a rapid tour through roughly eighty years of history. Kings rise and fall. Dynasties appear and disappear. In the north, the throne becomes a revolving door of violence—one king after another seizes power, commits the same sins as his predecessor, gets a prophetic death sentence, and is replaced by someone even worse. In the south, things are more stable, but the rot is creeping in there too.

It's a depressing stretch of history. But the writer isn't telling it to depress you. He's telling it to show you one thing:

through every failed king, every bloody coup, and every broken dynasty, God's word keeps coming true. Prophets speak. History obeys. And underneath all the chaos, God is working out a plan that no human king can derail.

JEROBOAM'S LAST CHANCE

The slide begins with a sick child. Jeroboam's son Abijah fell seriously ill. Despite everything—the golden calves, the counterfeit worship, the refusal to repent after the altar split at Bethel—Jeroboam still knew, deep down, where real answers came from. He sent his wife to the prophet Ahijah, the same man who had torn a cloak into twelve pieces and handed him ten. If anyone could tell him whether his son would recover, it was the prophet who had launched his career.

But Jeroboam didn't go himself. He knew he'd get an earful about the calves. So he sent his wife in disguise (different clothes, no royal markers) hoping the old prophet would think she was just an ordinary Israelite mother worried about a sick boy. Maybe then he'd get a favorable word.

There was just one problem with the plan. Two problems, actually. First, Ahijah was nearly blind, so the disguise was pointless. Second, God told Ahijah exactly who was coming and why before she even knocked on the door.

When the old prophet heard footsteps, he didn't wait for introductions: "Come in, wife of Jeroboam. Why this pretense? I have been sent to you with bad news."

God cannot be tricked. You can change your clothes, hide your identity, and rehearse your lines, but you cannot manipulate a word from the God who sees everything. Jeroboam wanted the help of God's word in his crisis but had rejected the rule of God's word over his life. He wanted to visit God in emergencies but had no interest in living with God day to day.

The message Ahijah delivered was devastating. He laid out the accusation like a prosecutor: "I raised you up from among the people. I made you leader over Israel. I tore the kingdom away from the house of David and gave it to you. But you have not been like my servant David. You have done more evil than all who lived before you. You have made other gods and metal images to provoke me, and me you have thrown behind your back."

Behind your back. That's where Jeroboam put the God who had given him everything. Not openly rejected—just casually set aside, like something you don't need anymore.

The sentence: Jeroboam's entire dynasty would be wiped out. Every male descendant. No proper burials. Dogs and vultures would handle that. As for the sick boy? He was the only one in Jeroboam's family in whom God found "something good." He would die, but he would be the only one to receive an honorable burial. His death was actually a mercy, sparing him from the bloodbath to come.

The moment Jeroboam's wife stepped across the threshold of their home in Tirzah, the boy died. Exactly as the prophet said.

But Ahijah wasn't finished. His prophecy extended far beyond Jeroboam's family. Because of the sins Jeroboam had introduced—the calves, the high places, the false priests—the entire northern kingdom was doomed. One day God would uproot Israel from the land and scatter them beyond the Euphrates River. Two hundred years later, the Assyrians would do exactly that.

The death of the boy was a sign. If the near prediction came true—and it did, that very day—then the far prediction was equally certain. God's word doesn't have an expiration date.

MEANWHILE IN JUDAH

The writer now turns south to give us a snapshot of what's happening in Judah under Rehoboam and his immediate successors. The picture isn't pretty, but it's different from the north in one crucial way.

Rehoboam reigned seventeen years, and Judah "did evil in the eyes of the LORD." They built high places, set up sacred stones and Asherah poles, and even tolerated shrine prostitutes. In short, they adopted the very practices of the nations God had driven out before them. The writer notes that Shishak, pharaoh of Egypt, invaded Jerusalem during Rehoboam's reign and carried off the treasures of the temple and the royal palace, including the gold shields Solomon had made. Rehoboam replaced them with bronze ones. It's a small detail, but it tells the whole story: the gold was gone. The glory was fading. Bronze substitutes for gold. That's what decline looks like.

After Rehoboam came his son Abijam, who reigned only three years and continued in "all the sins his father had committed before him." His heart, the text says, "was not fully devoted to the LORD his God, as the heart of David his forefather had been."

So why didn't God wipe out Judah the way he was about to wipe out Jeroboam's dynasty? The writer answers directly: "Nevertheless, for David's sake, the LORD his God gave him a lamp in Jerusalem by raising up a son to succeed him and by making Jerusalem strong. For David had done what was right in the eyes of the LORD and had not failed to keep any of the LORD's commands all the days of his life—except in the case of Uriah the Hittite."

There it is—the lamp. It's the same image God used when he told Solomon the kingdom would be torn: one tribe would remain "so that David my servant may always have a lamp before me in Jerusalem." Even when David's descendants were unfaithful, God kept the light burning. Not because they deserved it—Abijam certainly didn't—but because God had made a promise to David that he refused to break.

This is the fundamental difference between north and south. In the north, dynasties rise and fall based on each king's faithfulness. In the south, the line of David endures despite the kings' failures, because God's unconditional promise is stronger than human sin.

It's not that sin doesn't matter. The consequences are real: lost treasures, military defeats, spiritual decay. But the dynasty survives. The lamp stays lit.

A BRIGHT SPOT NAMED ASA

Then, unexpectedly, light broke through. Asa became king of Judah around 910 BC, and for the first time since the kingdom split, a king "did what was right in the eyes of the LORD, as his father David had done." After a parade of bad kings, those words land like a glass of cold water on a scorching day.

Asa was serious. He expelled the shrine prostitutes. He removed the idols his predecessors had made. He even deposed his own grandmother Maacah from her position as queen mother because she had made a "repulsive image" for the goddess Asherah. Asa cut the thing down and burned it in the Kidron Valley. When your reform extends to stripping your own grandmother of her royal title, people know you mean business.

The text does note a limitation: "Although he did not remove the high places, Asa's heart was fully committed to the LORD all his life." He wasn't perfect. The reform was incomplete. But his heart was pointed in the right direction, and that made him different from every king Judah had seen since Solomon.

Asa's reign wasn't all spiritual courage, though. When Baasha of Israel started fortifying Ramah—a city dangerously close to Jerusalem—as an economic blockade, Asa panicked. Instead of trusting God, he emptied the temple treasury and sent a massive bribe to Ben-hadad, king of Damascus, asking him to break his treaty with Baasha and attack Israel from the north. It worked. Baasha pulled back. Asa grabbed Baasha's building materials and used them to fortify his own border towns.

Brilliant politics. Terrible theology. Asa used temple gold to buy a pagan king's loyalty. The parallel account in 2 Chronicles tells us a prophet confronted him for relying on Damascus instead of God. But in 1 Kings, the writer lets Asa's own words do the condemning: he sent Ben-hadad "a bribe"—using the actual word for a corrupt payment. Success and faithfulness, it turns out, don't always go together.

Still, Asa's reign was a mercy. He proved that even in a downward spiral, God can raise up someone who slows the slide. Reform is possible. Faithfulness can appear even in dark times.

THE NORTHERN REVOLVING DOOR

Now buckle up, because the writer is about to sprint through a series of northern kings so fast it will make your head spin. And that's the point. The rapid pace tells you something about the nature of these reigns: they are brief, violent, and repetitive.

Nadab, Jeroboam's son, took the throne and reigned two years. He "did evil in the eyes of the LORD, walking in the ways of his father." Then Baasha conspired against him, assassinated him during a military siege, and wiped out every last member of Jeroboam's family, "just as the word of the LORD had declared through his servant Ahijah the Shilonite." Ahijah's prophecy, delivered to Jeroboam's wife, came true to the letter.

Did Baasha learn anything from destroying a dynasty that God had condemned for idolatry? He did not. He reigned twenty-four years and "did evil in the eyes of the LORD, walking in the ways of Jeroboam and in his sin." Same golden calves. Same false worship. Same verdict. A prophet named Jehu delivered the same doom over Baasha's house that Ahijah had delivered over Jeroboam's: total destruction, no proper burials, dogs and vultures.

Baasha's son Elah lasted two years before one of his own officials, a chariot commander named Zimri, murdered him while he was getting drunk at a party. Zimri then slaughtered Baasha's entire family—again, "in accordance with the word of the LORD spoken against Baasha through the prophet Jehu." Another prophecy fulfilled. Another dynasty erased.

But Zimri's reign was the shortest of all: seven days. When the Israelite army heard about the coup, they proclaimed their commander Omri as king and marched on the capital. Zimri saw the city was lost, walked into the royal palace, set it on fire, and died in the flames. Seven days from coup to cremation.

After a civil war between Omri's supporters and a rival named Tibni, Omri emerged as king and reigned twelve years. The writer's summary is brief and brutal: "Omri did evil in the eyes of the LORD and sinned more than all those before him." Each new king doesn't just match the previous evil—he exceeds it. The bar keeps dropping.

Omri's one notable accomplishment was buying a hill and building a new capital city: Samaria. It would become the permanent seat of the northern kingdom and eventually give its name to the whole region. But from the writer's perspective, even a brilliant piece of urban planning doesn't matter if you're leading people away from God.

THE WORST OF ALL

And then came Ahab. If each northern king was worse than the last, Ahab was the one who broke the scale. "Ahab son of Omri did more evil in the eyes of the LORD than any of those before him." The writer repeats it for emphasis: "He did more to arouse the anger of the LORD, the God of Israel, than did all the kings of Israel before him."

What made Ahab uniquely terrible? Three things.

First, he continued the sins of Jeroboam—the golden calves, the high places, all of it. But the text asks, almost sarcastically, whether that wasn't bad enough by itself.

Second, he married Jezebel, daughter of Ethbaal, king of the Sidonians. Jezebel wasn't content to practice her religion privately. She was an aggressive evangelist for Baal worship, a driving force who would systematically hunt down and murder God's prophets. She would become the most infamous queen in Israel's history.

Third, Ahab built a temple for Baal in Samaria and erected an Asherah pole. Under Jeroboam, Israel worshiped God in the wrong way: golden calves instead of the temple. Under Ahab, Israel worshiped the wrong god entirely. The calves were bad. Baal was catastrophically worse.

The writer closes his introduction to Ahab with a chilling detail. During Ahab's reign, a man from Bethel named Hiel rebuilt the fortress of Jericho. When he laid the foundation, his firstborn son died. When he set up the city gates, his youngest son died. This happened "in accordance with the word of the LORD spoken by Joshua son of Nun"—a curse Joshua had pronounced over five hundred years earlier.

Five hundred years. And God's word still stood. It didn't matter how many centuries had passed. What God said would happen, happened.

That detail tells you everything about the era of Ahab. This was a time when people thought nothing of defying God's word—and discovered that God's word defied back.

WHAT THIS MEANS FOR US

First, you can't manipulate God. Jeroboam tried to trick the prophet with a disguise. It didn't work. God sees through every pretense. He's not interested in our performances. He wants our honesty.

Second, sin is boring. Did you notice how repetitive these chapters are? "He did evil in the eyes of the LORD, walking in the ways of Jeroboam." Over and over. Sin never produces anything original. It just copies and repeats. Faithfulness is creative; rebellion is a broken record.

Third, God keeps his promises on both sides. He promised to destroy Jeroboam's house—and he did. He promised to preserve David's line—and he did. God is faithful in judgment and faithful in mercy. Both are equally certain.

Fourth, reform is always possible. Asa's reign proves that even in a long downward slide, God can raise up someone who turns things around. The situation is never so hopeless that faithfulness becomes pointless.

Fifth, evil can always get worse. Each northern king exceeded the one before. The writer wants us to understand that there is no floor to how bad things can get when people abandon God. But he also wants us to know that God is never caught off guard. He always knows exactly how bad it is—and he always has a plan.

TALKING POINTS

1. **Jeroboam wanted God's help in a crisis but didn't want God's rule in everyday life.** Have you ever been tempted to pray only when things go wrong? What's the difference between visiting God and living with him?

2. **Rehoboam replaced Solomon's gold shields with bronze ones.** What are some ways we settle for "bronze" versions of what God offers?

3. **Asa was faithful in worship but relied on a bribe instead of God when he faced a political crisis.** Why is it some-

times easier to trust God in "religious" areas than in practical, everyday problems?

4. **The northern kings repeat the same sins over and over.** Why do you think people keep making the same mistakes even when they can see the consequences in others?

5. **The writer says Ahab was worse than all who came before him.** How does evil grow over time when it goes unchecked?

Eighty years of history. A dozen kings. Dynasties rising and crashing. And through it all, God's word—spoken through prophets like Ahijah and Jehu—comes true every single time. The altar splits. The boy dies. The dynasty falls. The fortress builder buries his sons. Every prophecy lands.

But the darkest hour is also the setup for the greatest showdown in the Old Testament. Because Ahab and Jezebel are about to meet someone they didn't see coming. From the wilderness of Gilead, a prophet is on his way. His name means "My God is the LORD."

Turn the page.

7

THE PROPHET FROM NOWHERE

In *The Lord of the Rings*, there's a moment when everything looks hopeless. The fortress of Helm's Deep is surrounded. The walls have been breached. The defenders are exhausted, outnumbered, and running out of time. King Théoden looks at the wreckage and says, "So much death. What can men do against such reckless hate?"

And then, at first light on the fifth day, Gandalf appears on the ridge with an army of riders behind him. He arrives exactly when he said he would, and the battle turns.

That's 1 Kings 17. The kingdom is overrun. Baal worship has invaded every corner of Israelite life. Queen Jezebel is systematically murdering God's prophets. King Ahab has built a temple for Baal in Samaria. The situation looks hopeless.

And then, without warning, a prophet appears out of nowhere. No introduction. No backstory. No family tree. Just a man from the wilderness of Gilead who walks into Ahab's court and announces that the sky is about to shut.

His name is Elijah. It means "My God is the LORD." And

the next two chapters of 1 Kings are the most dramatic showdown in the entire Old Testament.

THE PROPHET FROM NOWHERE

Elijah's entrance is one of the most abrupt in all of Scripture. The writer doesn't ease us into it. There's no "Now there was a man in Gilead named Elijah, and the word of the LORD came to him." Instead, Elijah simply appears in front of Ahab and delivers a single devastating sentence: "As the LORD, the God of Israel, lives, whom I serve, there will be neither dew nor rain in the next few years except at my word."

Then he's gone. No debate. No negotiation. Just a proclamation and a disappearance.

Think about what Elijah was really saying. Baal was supposed to be the storm god—the one who sent rain, who made crops grow, who kept the land fertile. Baal's whole reputation depended on weather. If Elijah was right and the rain stopped, it would mean one of two things: either Baal couldn't send rain, or someone more powerful than Baal had turned the faucet off. Either way, Baal was exposed.

The drought was a direct challenge: Let's see what your fertility god does when the sky goes silent.

RAVENS AND A WIDOW

God told Elijah to hide by a brook east of the Jordan, and promised that ravens would bring him food. Ravens—scavenger birds that Israelites considered unclean. Not exactly the catering service you'd request. But every morning and every evening, those dirty birds showed up with bread and meat. God doesn't always provide through the channels we'd choose.

When the brook dried up, God sent Elijah somewhere even more surprising: Zarephath, a town in Sidon, and Jezebel's home territory. Baal's backyard. And the person God designated to feed his prophet wasn't a wealthy donor or a powerful ally. It was a widow on the verge of starvation.

When Elijah found her, she was gathering sticks to cook one final meal for herself and her son. "I have nothing baked," she told him. "Only a handful of flour in a jar and a little olive oil in a jug. I am gathering a few sticks to take home and make a meal for myself and my son, that we may eat it—and die."

Elijah's response sounds almost cruel: "Don't be afraid. Go home and do as you have said. But first make a small loaf of bread for me."

First? She was about to cook her last meal, and this stranger wanted to eat before she did? But Elijah didn't stop there. He gave her a promise: "For this is what the LORD, the God of Israel, says: 'The jar of flour will not be used up and the jug of oil will not run dry until the day the LORD sends rain on the land.'"

The widow had a choice. She could hold onto what little she had—a handful of flour and a final supper—or she could gamble everything on the word of a God she barely knew.

She chose to trust. She went home and made bread for Elijah first. And the jar of flour did not run out. The jug of oil did not run dry. Day after day, morning after morning, she went to the cupboard and found just enough for another day. Not a surplus. Not bags of grain stacked against the wall. Just enough—every single day—exactly as God's word had promised.

This is what faith looks like in its simplest form: staking everything on the sheer word of God, even when there's no visible evidence that it will work.

LIFE FROM DEATH

Then the widow's son got sick and died. Imagine her confusion. She had trusted this prophet. She had watched God provide day after day. And now her only son was dead in her arms. She turned on Elijah: "What do you have against me, man of God? Did you come to remind God of my sin and kill my son?"

Her words reflect what grief does to faith—it scrambles our theology. She knew Elijah was a man of God. She had experienced God's provision firsthand. But death made her wonder if God's attention had become dangerous rather than helpful.

Elijah didn't argue with her. He took the boy, carried him upstairs, laid him on the bed, and cried out to God: "LORD my God, have you brought tragedy even on this widow I am staying with, by causing her son to die?" Then he stretched himself over the boy three times and prayed: "LORD my God, let this boy's life return to him!"

And God heard. The boy's life returned, and Elijah carried him downstairs and placed him in his mother's arms.

This was the ultimate proof. Baal supposedly controlled fertility and life. In Canaanite mythology, Baal periodically lost his battle with Mot (the god of death) and had to be revived. But the God of Israel didn't bargain with death or lose to it. He simply commanded life to return, and it did. No ritual. No struggle. Just a prayer and a resurrection.

The widow's response was total conviction: "Now I know

that you are a man of God and that the word of the LORD from your mouth is the truth."

THE SECRET AGENT

Three years into the drought, God told Elijah it was time to go back. But before the big showdown, the writer introduces us to someone unexpected: Obadiah, Ahab's chief of staff.

Obadiah was a devout worshiper of the LORD, right in the heart of Ahab's government. When Jezebel was slaughtering God's prophets, Obadiah had hidden a hundred of them in caves, fifty to a cave, and supplied them with bread and water. He risked his career and his life to protect God's servants, and he did it all quietly, behind the scenes, without anyone making a movie about it.

The writer pairs Obadiah and Elijah deliberately. Elijah is the public confronter—bold, dramatic, in your face. Obadiah is the quiet subversive—faithful in a hostile environment, doing what he can where God placed him. Both are servants of God. Both are essential. Not everyone is called to stand on a mountain and call down fire. Some are called to hide prophets in caves and keep them alive with bread and water.

Meanwhile, Ahab was out searching for grass to keep his horses and mules from dying. His wife was butchering prophets, but the king was worried about livestock. That single detail tells you everything about Ahab's priorities.

When Elijah sent word through Obadiah that he was ready to meet the king, Ahab greeted him with a snarl: "Is that you, you troubler of Israel?"

Elijah didn't flinch: "I have not made trouble for Israel. But you have. You have abandoned the LORD's commands and have followed the Baals."

Then Elijah issued his challenge: "Summon the people from all over Israel to meet me on Mount Carmel. And bring the four hundred and fifty prophets of Baal."

THE SHOWDOWN ON CARMEL

Mount Carmel juts out toward the Mediterranean Sea in northern Israel. Ancient records suggest it was considered sacred to Baal, his home turf. If Elijah was going to prove that the Lord was God, he would do it on the other team's home court.

The setup was simple. Two altars. Two bulls. No fire. The god who answers by sending fire from heaven is the real God.

But first, Elijah addressed the crowd with one of the most famous questions in the Bible: "How long will you waver between two opinions? If the LORD is God, follow him; but if Baal is God, follow him."

The people said nothing. Their silence was the sound of a nation that had been hedging its bets—worshiping Baal when it was convenient, claiming loyalty to the Lord when it was safe, and never actually committing to either one.

Elijah let the prophets of Baal go first. They chose their bull, prepared it on the altar, and began calling on Baal. They called all morning. Nothing happened. They danced around the altar in frantic worship. Nothing. They shouted louder.

At noon, Elijah started taunting them—and the mockery is one of the funniest moments in the Bible: "Shout louder! Surely he is a god! Perhaps he is deep in thought, or busy, or traveling. Maybe he is sleeping and must be awakened." The word translated "busy" may actually be a crude reference to Baal using the bathroom. Elijah was mocking their god with bathroom humor on national television.

The prophets of Baal responded by shouting louder, slashing themselves with swords and spears until blood flowed—a common practice in pagan worship, trying desperately to get their god's attention through self-inflicted pain. The text says they carried on "until the time for the evening sacrifice." They had been at it for hours.

And the verdict: "There was no response, no one answered, no one paid attention." Three devastating phrases. No response. No answer. No attention. Baal wasn't busy or traveling or asleep. Baal wasn't there. Baal was nothing.

THE GOD WHO ANSWERS

Then it was Elijah's turn. He called the people closer. He wanted witnesses. He rebuilt an altar to the Lord that had been torn down, using twelve stones, one for each tribe of Israel. Even in the divided kingdom, God still saw twelve tribes, one people.

Then Elijah did something astonishing. He drenched the sacrifice with water. Not once but three times. He filled a trench around the altar until it was overflowing. In the middle of a drought, when water was precious, Elijah soaked everything so thoroughly that no one could accuse him of trickery. He was making the impossible even more impossible.

Then he prayed. No shouting. No dancing. No bloodletting. Just a simple, direct prayer: "LORD, the God of Abraham, Isaac and Israel, let it be known today that you are God in Israel and that I am your servant and have done all these things at your command. Answer me, LORD, answer me, so these people will know that you, LORD, are God, and that you are turning their hearts back again."

That's it. No frenzy. No performance. Just a man talking to his God.

And fire fell. Not a small flame. Fire from heaven that burned up the sacrifice, the wood, the stones, the soil, and even licked up the water in the trench. Everything. Gone.

The people hit the ground: "The LORD—he is God! The LORD—he is God!"

Four hundred and fifty prophets of Baal were seized and executed at the Kishon Valley. The contest was over.

RAIN

But Elijah wasn't done. Fire had proven who God was. Now rain would prove that God provides.

Elijah sent Ahab to eat and drink while he climbed to the top of Carmel, crouched down with his face between his knees, and prayed. He sent his servant to look toward the sea. "There is nothing," the servant reported. Elijah sent him back. Seven times the servant went and looked, and six times the answer was the same: nothing.

On the seventh trip: "A cloud as small as a man's hand is rising from the sea." That was enough. Elijah sent word to Ahab: "Hitch up your chariot and go down before the rain stops you."

The sky grew black with clouds. Wind came. And then the rain—a heavy, drenching, life-giving rain. Three and a half years of silence, and the heavens opened.

Then Elijah, empowered by God's hand, hiked up his robe

and ran ahead of Ahab's chariot all the way to Jezreel (roughly seventeen miles). The prophet running before the king was a picture of what should have been: God's word leading the king, the king following the prophet, the nation restored.

For one shining moment, it seemed like everything might be set right.

WHAT THIS MEANS FOR US

First, God shows up when things look darkest. Elijah appeared at the worst moment in Israel's history. When evil seems unstoppable, God is already preparing his response. The situation is never as hopeless as it looks.

Second, faith means trusting God's word before you see the results. The widow fed Elijah before she saw the flour replenished. She gambled on God's promise when her cupboard was nearly empty. Faith isn't waiting until you have proof. It's acting on God's word before the proof arrives.

Third, faithful service comes in different forms. Elijah confronted kings on mountaintops. Obadiah hid prophets in caves. Both were essential. God doesn't call everyone to the same kind of service, and the quiet work of faithfulness is just as vital as the dramatic moments.

Fourth, the real God doesn't need our frantic efforts. The contrast between Baal's prophets and Elijah is stunning. Hours of screaming, dancing, and bloodletting produced nothing. One calm prayer produced fire from heaven. God's power doesn't depend on our intensity. It depends on his character.

Fifth, God provides, but not always the way we expect. Ravens. A starving widow. A jar that never empties. God's provision often comes through channels we wouldn't choose, in amounts that are just enough, through people we wouldn't have picked. But it comes.

TALKING POINTS

1. **Elijah appeared out of nowhere at Israel's darkest moment.** Can you think of times when help or hope showed up when you least expected it?
2. **The widow had to feed Elijah before she saw the miracle.** Why does God sometimes ask us to act in faith before showing us the results?
3. **Elijah was the public hero.** Obadiah was the behind-the-scenes servant. Which role do you think is harder? Which would you prefer?
4. **The prophets of Baal worked themselves into a frenzy trying to get their god's attention.** Elijah simply prayed. What does that contrast teach us about what God is really like?
5. **The people said, "The LORD—he is God!" but the very next chapter shows how fragile that commitment was.** Why is one dramatic experience usually not enough to change someone permanently?

Fire and rain. A dead god exposed and a living God revealed. A soaked altar consumed and a parched land drenched. It was the single greatest day in the history of the northern kingdom. But the queen wasn't on the mountain that day. And she wasn't impressed with the results.

Turn the page.

8

THE DAY AFTER

In *Inside Out*, eleven-year-old Riley's emotions—Joy, Sadness, Fear, Anger, and Disgust—run the control panel in her brain. Joy tries to keep things positive all the time, but the real turning point of the movie happens when Riley finally breaks down. She stops running, stops pretending everything is fine, and lets herself feel the sadness she's been stuffing down. That's when her parents hold her close. That's when healing begins. Not during a victory. After a collapse.

First Kings 19 is the Bible's version of that moment. One chapter ago, Elijah was standing on a mountaintop watching fire fall from heaven. The people were shouting, "The LORD—he is God!" Rain was pouring down after three and a half years of drought. It was the greatest spiritual victory in Israel's history.

And now? Now the prophet is sitting under a bush in the desert, alone, begging God to let him die.

This chapter isn't about a prophet losing his faith. It's about what God does when his servant has nothing left.

THE THREAT

Everything unraveled with a single message. Ahab went home and told Jezebel what had happened on Mount Carmel—all of it. The fire, the rain, the slaughter of her 450 prophets of Baal. And Jezebel, who had not been on the mountain that day, sent a messenger to Elijah with an oath: "May the gods deal with me, be it ever so severely, if by this time tomorrow I do not make your life like that of one of them."

Think about what this meant. The entire nation had just witnessed Baal exposed as a fraud. Fire had fallen from heaven. The people had confessed that the Lord was God. And none of it mattered to Jezebel. She wasn't shaken. She wasn't reconsidering. She was doubling down.

Elijah saw the situation clearly: nothing was going to change. Jezebel still ran the kingdom. Ahab was still her puppet. The people's confession on Carmel was already evaporating. One woman's stubborn refusal to bow had undone the greatest miracle in living memory.

So Elijah ran. He fled south—far south—past Beersheba at the bottom of Judah, a hundred miles from Jezebel. Then he left his servant behind and went another day's journey into the wilderness alone. He sat down under a broom tree and prayed a prayer that might shock you: "I have had enough, LORD. Take my life; I am no better than my ancestors."

This wasn't fear of Jezebel. By the time he reached the desert, he was well out of her reach. This was something deeper. Elijah was broken. He had given everything to God's cause—years of hiding, the confrontation on Carmel, the emotional and physical exhaustion of that day—and it hadn't been enough. Israel was still in Jezebel's grip. The prophet who had called down fire from heaven now lay under a scraggly bush and asked to die.

BREAD AND SLEEP

God's response to Elijah's despair was not a lecture. It was a nap and a meal. Elijah fell asleep under the tree, and an angel touched him and said, "Get up and eat." When he opened his eyes, he found bread baked over hot coals and a jar of water sitting by his head. He ate, drank, and lay back down.

The angel came a second time: "Get up and eat, for the journey is too much for you."

Notice what God didn't do. He didn't scold Elijah for running. He didn't say, "What happened to your faith?" He didn't deliver a theological lecture about courage. He fed him. Twice. Sometimes what a broken person needs isn't a sermon—it's sleep and bread and someone who shows up without demanding an explanation.

Strengthened by that food, Elijah traveled forty days and forty nights until he reached Horeb, the mountain of God.

Horeb. Also called Sinai. The mountain where God had given Moses the covenant. The mountain where Israel was born as a nation. The mountain where God's presence had descended in fire, cloud, and thunder. Elijah wasn't wandering aimlessly. He was going back to the beginning, back to the place where everything started between God and his people.

THE CAVE AND THE QUESTION

When Elijah arrived, he went into a cave and spent the night.

Then the word of the Lord came to him with a simple question: "What are you doing here, Elijah?"

Many people read that question as a rebuke, as if God were scolding him for being in the wrong place. But consider the context. God's own angel had fed Elijah for the journey. God had sustained him for forty days of travel. It seems more likely that this was an invitation rather than an accusation—like a father saying, "Tell me what's on your heart."

Elijah poured it out: "I have been very zealous for the LORD God Almighty. The Israelites have rejected your covenant, torn down your altars, and put your prophets to death with the sword. I am the only one left, and now they are trying to kill me too."

Was Elijah exaggerating? A little—Obadiah had hidden a hundred prophets in caves, so Elijah wasn't literally the last one standing. But the substance of his complaint was accurate. Israel had broken the covenant. Altars had been torn down. Prophets had been murdered. And after everything God did on Carmel, nothing had fundamentally changed. Elijah wasn't whining about a failed career. He was filing a formal report: God's people had broken God's covenant, and the evidence was overwhelming.

WIND, EARTHQUAKE, FIRE—AND SILENCE

God told Elijah to go stand on the mountain, "for the LORD is about to pass by."

What happened next echoed Moses' own experience on this same mountain centuries earlier. A great and powerful wind tore the mountains apart and shattered rocks. But the

Lord was not in the wind. Then an earthquake. But the Lord was not in the earthquake. Then fire. But the Lord was not in the fire.

Wind. Earthquake. Fire. These were the kinds of dramatic displays Elijah had seen God use before—fire falling on Carmel, storms breaking the drought. But God was not in any of them this time.

And after the fire came a gentle whisper. When Elijah heard it, he pulled his cloak over his face, stepped out of the cave, and stood at the entrance. He knew. This was God.

Why a whisper? After all the fireworks on Carmel, why would God reveal himself in near-silence? Maybe because Elijah needed to learn that God doesn't always work through the spectacular. The fire on Carmel had been dramatic, public, undeniable—and it hadn't permanently changed anyone's heart. Jezebel shrugged it off. The people's commitment evaporated. Perhaps God was showing Elijah that his kingdom doesn't always advance through explosive displays of power. Sometimes it advances quietly—through a faithful remnant, a whispered word, a still presence in the dark.

God asked the same question again: "What are you doing here, Elijah?" And Elijah gave the same answer, word for word. He wasn't being stubborn. He was telling the truth.

THE ASSIGNMENT

And God agreed with him. God didn't rebuke Elijah's assessment. He didn't say, "You're wrong about Israel." Instead, he essentially said, "You're right. And here's what I'm going to do about it."

God gave Elijah three assignments. First, anoint Hazael as king over Aram (Syria). Second, anoint Jehu as king over Israel. Third, anoint Elisha as prophet to succeed Elijah himself. These three—a foreign king, a new Israelite king, and a new prophet—would be God's instruments of judgment on the house of Ahab. The verdict Elijah had brought against Israel at Horeb would be carried out, but through agents God would raise up over time.

Then came the final word, and it changed everything: "Yet I reserve seven thousand in Israel, all whose knees have not bowed down to Baal and all whose mouths have not kissed him."

Seven thousand. Elijah thought he was alone. He wasn't. God had been quietly preserving a faithful remnant all along—people Elijah had never met, people who had resisted the pressure to conform, people whose names would never make it into a Bible story but whose knees had never touched the ground in front of a golden calf.

Elijah couldn't see them. But God could. And God was keeping them.

THE FARM BOY

Elijah obeyed. He left Horeb and found Elisha son of Shaphat plowing a field with twelve pairs of oxen. No warning. No appointment. Elijah simply walked across the field and threw his cloak over Elisha's shoulders.

Elisha understood immediately. The mantle was the prophetic uniform. Receiving it meant receiving the call. He asked only for permission to kiss his parents goodbye, then went home and did something remarkable. He slaughtered his oxen, burned his plowing equipment to cook the meat, and threw a farewell feast for the community.

Burning the plow was the point. Elisha wasn't keeping a backup plan. He wasn't thinking, "If this prophet thing doesn't work out, I can always go back to farming." He destroyed his old life so there was nothing to go back to. Then he set out to follow Elijah and became his servant.

Not his co-star. His servant. The man God had chosen to carry on the prophetic mission started his new life by pouring water on Elijah's hands.

WHAT THIS MEANS FOR US

First, victory doesn't make you invincible. The day after Elijah's greatest triumph was the day he fell apart. Emotional and spiritual crashes often follow mountain-top experiences. If you've ever felt empty after something amazing, you're in good company.

Second, God meets broken people with kindness, not criticism. Bread, water, sleep, and a gentle voice. That was God's prescription for a shattered prophet. Sometimes the most spiritual thing you can do is eat a meal and rest.

Third, God is not limited to the dramatic. Wind, earthquake, and fire are impressive, but God spoke in the whisper. His most important work often happens quietly, in ordinary faithfulness that nobody films or applauds.

Fourth, you are never as alone as you feel. Elijah was convinced he was the last faithful person on earth. God had seven thousand others he didn't know about. When you feel like you're the only one who cares, remember: God sees people you can't.

Fifth, saying yes to God's call means letting go. Elisha burned his plow. Following God always costs something: comfort, familiarity, a backup plan. But Elisha didn't mourn what he left behind. He threw a party.

TALKING POINTS

1. **Elijah's lowest moment came right after his greatest victory.** Why do you think high points are often followed by low points?
2. **God responded to Elijah's despair with food and rest instead of a rebuke.** What does that tell you about how God treats people who are struggling?
3. **God wasn't in the wind, earthquake, or fire—he was in the whisper.** What are some "quiet" ways God might work in people's lives today?
4. **Elijah thought he was alone, but God had seven thousand faithful people he didn't know about.** Have you ever felt like you were the only one doing the right thing?
5. **Elisha burned his plowing equipment when he accepted God's call.** What would it look like for someone your age to follow God without a backup plan?

Elijah left Horeb with three assignments, a successor walking behind him, and the knowledge that seven thousand faithful people were out there somewhere. God wasn't finished with Israel. But Israel wasn't finished with Ahab, either. The king who had stood silent on Mount Carmel and watched fire fall from heaven was about to prove that witnessing a miracle and learning from it are two very different things. Wars were coming.

So was an innocent man's blood on the ground. And the word of God would track Ahab down in the last place he expected.

Turn the page.

9

THE KING WHO COULDN'T SAY NO

In the first *Despicable Me* movie, Gru is supposed to be the villain. He's got the lair, the minions, the freeze ray, the master plan. But the moment those three orphan girls show up, you realize something: Gru is soft. He can't say no to them. He can't say no to the cookie sales, the amusement park trips, or the bedtime stories. His villain reputation is a costume he wears over a man who is constantly being pushed around by whoever is standing in front of him.

Ahab is a lot like that—minus the heartwarming ending.

On the surface, Ahab is the most powerful man in Israel. He commands armies, builds cities, and sits on a throne. But when you watch him in action across 1 Kings 20–21, a pattern emerges. He does whatever the last person told him to do. A prophet gives an order? Ahab obeys. A defeated enemy proposes a treaty? Ahab agrees. His wife tells him to stop moping and let her handle things? Ahab rolls over and lets it happen. He's a king who can't say no to anyone—and that weakness will cost innocent people their lives and seal the doom of his entire dynasty.

TWO WARS AHAB DIDN'T START

Chapter 20 opens with a surprise. Ben-hadad, king of Aram (Syria), marches on Samaria with a coalition of thirty-two kings and puts Ahab's capital under siege. His demands are outrageous: first he wants Ahab's silver, gold, wives, and children as tribute. Ahab meekly agrees. Then Ben-hadad ups the ante: his men will come search Ahab's palace and take whatever they want. That finally pushes Ahab to resist.

Here's where it gets unexpected. A prophet—not Elijah, but an unnamed prophet—approaches Ahab with a message from God: "Do you see this vast army? I will give it into your hand today, and then you will know that I am the LORD."

Wait. God is helping Ahab? The same Ahab who built a temple for Baal? The same king whose wife slaughtered God's prophets? Yes. And God didn't wait for Ahab to ask. The prophet came unsolicited, bringing a word of promise that Ahab had done nothing to earn.

Following the prophet's instructions, Ahab sent out a small force of young officers who caught Ben-hadad's army off guard (partly because the Syrian king was drunk at the time). Israel won a stunning victory, and Ben-hadad barely escaped on horseback.

The prophet returned with a warning: "Strengthen your position. The king of Aram will attack you again next spring."

Sure enough, the Syrians regrouped. Their military advisors came up with a theory: "Israel's gods are gods of the hills. That's why they beat us. If we fight them on the plains, we'll win." Bad theology produces bad strategy. God is not limited to certain geography. He had already demonstrated his power in Phoenician territory (with the widow), on Carmel (with the fire), and in the desert (with Elijah). The whole earth belongs to him.

When the Syrians attacked again, another prophet delivered another promise: "Because the Arameans think the LORD is a god of the hills and not of the valleys, I will deliver this vast army into your hands, and you will know that I am the LORD."

Israel won again, devastatingly. The wall of the city of Aphek collapsed on the retreating Syrian soldiers, an echo of Jericho's walls falling in the days of Joshua. God was fighting for Israel the same way he always had.

Then Ahab made his fatal mistake.

THE KING WHO LET THE ENEMY GO

Ben-hadad surrendered. His officials dressed in sackcloth and ropes and came groveling to Ahab: "Your servant Ben-hadad says, 'Please let me live.'" And Ahab, instead of treating this as a holy war in which God had devoted the enemy to destruction, called Ben-hadad "my brother," invited him into his chariot, and struck a business deal. In exchange for some cities and trading rights in Damascus, Ahab let Ben-hadad walk free.

It was a savvy political move. It was a catastrophic spiritual failure.

The pattern in Israel's history was clear. When God gave an enemy into your hand and declared that enemy devoted to destruction, you didn't get to renegotiate the terms. King Saul had made this exact mistake centuries earlier when he spared Agag, king of the Amalekites, after God had ordered total destruction. That act of "mercy" cost Saul his throne. Now Ahab repeated Saul's sin.

God sent another prophet to confront the king. Through a clever ruse—disguising himself, pretending to be a soldier who had lost a prisoner—the prophet tricked Ahab into pronouncing his own sentence. When the disguise came off, the prophet delivered God's verdict: "Because you have set free a man I had determined should die, it will be your life for his life, your people for his people."

Ahab went home to Samaria "sullen and angry." Not repentant. Not broken. Just irritated that God's word had once again gotten in his way. Remember that reaction. You'll see it again in the next chapter.

A VINEYARD AND A REFUSAL

Next door to Ahab's palace in Jezreel, a man named Naboth owned a vineyard. It had been in his family for generations—an inheritance from his ancestors, a piece of land that God had assigned to his family when Israel first entered the promised land.

Ahab wanted it. He offered Naboth a fair deal: a better vineyard in exchange, or a cash payment. It was a reasonable offer by the world's standards. But Naboth's answer was rooted in something deeper than economics: "The LORD forbid that I should give you the inheritance of my ancestors."

This wasn't stubbornness. Under Israelite law, the land God had given to families was supposed to stay in those families. It wasn't just real estate. It was a sign of God's covenant, a concrete reminder that God had given this people this land. Selling the family inheritance would be like tearing up a promise from God. Naboth refused because he feared God more than he feared the king.

Ahab went home, lay on his bed, turned his face to the wall, and refused to eat. The most powerful man in Israel was pouting like a child who didn't get the toy he wanted.

JEZEBEL TAKES OVER

This is where the story turns dark. Jezebel found her husband sulking and asked what was wrong. When he told her, her response dripped with contempt: "Is this how you act as king over Israel? Get up and eat! I'll get you the vineyard of Naboth."

Then she executed a plan that was as efficient as it was evil. She wrote letters in Ahab's name, sealed them with his royal seal, and sent them to the elders and nobles of Jezreel. The instructions were specific: proclaim a fast, seat Naboth in a prominent place, then hire two scoundrels to accuse him publicly of cursing God and the king. Once the false testimony was in place, take him outside the city and stone him to death.

Every step of the plan was followed to the letter. The writer tells it with a chilling matter-of-factness. Jezebel wrote this; the elders did that. Command and compliance, like a military operation. The city leaders of Jezreel knew exactly what was happening. They knew the charges were fabricated. They knew Naboth was innocent. And not one of them lifted a finger to stop it.

Naboth was stoned to death. Second Kings 9:26 tells us his sons were killed too—probably to prevent any heir from reclaiming the property. An entire family wiped out so that a king could have a vegetable garden.

When Jezebel got word that Naboth was dead, she told Ahab the vineyard was his. And Ahab—passive, sulking, spineless Ahab—got up and went down to take possession. He didn't ask how Jezebel had gotten it. He didn't want to know. He just took what his wife's violence had secured.

THE WORD THAT TRACKS YOU DOWN

It looked like the perfect crime. The letters had been shredded. The witnesses had been paid. The body was buried. No one in Jezreel was going to talk.

But God saw everything. "Then the word of the LORD came to Elijah the Tishbite: 'Go down to meet Ahab king of Israel, who rules in Samaria. He is now in Naboth's vineyard, where he has gone to take possession of it.'"

Elijah met Ahab in the stolen vineyard. Ahab's greeting was bitter: "So you have found me, my enemy!"

"I have found you," Elijah answered, "because you have sold yourself to do evil in the eyes of the LORD."

Then came the sentence. Because of what Ahab had done—because of the judicial murder, the stolen inheritance, and all the idolatry that had led to this moment—God would bring disaster on Ahab's house. His dynasty would be cut off completely, just like Jeroboam's and Baasha's before him. Dogs would devour Jezebel by the wall of Jezreel. Every member of Ahab's family would meet a violent end.

The writer pauses to editorialize, and the words are devastating: "There was never anyone like Ahab, who sold himself to do evil in the eyes of the LORD, urged on by Jezebel his wife."

"Sold himself." That's the language of slavery. Ahab had

become a slave to evil—not because he was a dramatic villain, but because he was a weak man who never said no. He never said no to Jezebel's Baal worship. He never said no to her scheme against Naboth. He never said no to the steady erosion of everything God's covenant stood for. His passivity was its own kind of wickedness.

A SURPRISE AT THE END

What happened next is one of the most unexpected moments in the entire book. When Ahab heard Elijah's sentence, he tore his clothes, put on sackcloth, fasted, and walked around in mourning.

And God noticed. He said to Elijah—almost with a tone of surprise—"Have you seen how Ahab has humbled himself before me? Because he has humbled himself, I will not bring this disaster in his day. I will bring it on his house in the days of his son."

Was Ahab's repentance real? It seems to have been genuine in the moment, even if it didn't last. The judgment wasn't canceled. It was postponed. Ahab's dynasty would still fall. But God, who had every reason to bring the hammer down immediately, chose to show mercy because a wicked king put on sackcloth and grieved.

That tells you something remarkable about God. He's not looking for an excuse to punish. He's looking for the faintest flicker of humility so he can extend grace. Even to an Ahab.

WHAT THIS MEANS FOR US

First, undeserved grace demands a response. God helped Ahab win two wars he didn't deserve to win. Grace that's received without gratitude eventually hardens into entitlement. When God is generous, it's an invitation to respond with worship, not a license to keep living the same way.

Second, passivity isn't innocence. Ahab didn't personally write the letters or hire the false witnesses. But he was guilty of Naboth's murder because he allowed it, benefited from it, and never tried to stop it. Doing nothing when you could do something is its own form of evil.

Third, no crime is hidden from God. Jezebel ran a clean operation. Not a single loose end. But God saw it all, and he sent his word to track Ahab down in the very vineyard where the injustice had been committed. You can fool courts and cover your tracks, but you cannot hide from the God who sees.

Fourth, God takes the side of the powerless. Naboth was one man against the monarchy. He lost. But God didn't let it stand. The story of Naboth's vineyard is a promise to every person who has ever been crushed by powerful people: God sees, God cares, and God will act.

Fifth, God's mercy is staggeringly generous. Even after everything Ahab did, a moment of genuine humility moved God to delay judgment. If God responds to Ahab's sackcloth, imagine what he'll do with sincere repentance.

TALKING POINTS

1. **Ahab let Ben-hadad go because it was politically smart, even though God had determined the king should be destroyed.** When is "smart" not the same as "right"?

2. **Naboth lost his life because he refused to sell his family's inheritance.** What are some things that should never be for sale, no matter the price?

3. **The elders of Jezreel knew Naboth was innocent but went along with Jezebel's plan anyway.** What makes it hard to stand up when powerful people are doing wrong?

4. **Ahab didn't directly kill Naboth, but God held him responsible.** When does staying silent or passive make you part of the problem?

5. **God showed mercy to Ahab when he humbled himself—even though Ahab's track record was terrible.** What does that tell you about how God responds to even small steps of repentance?

Ahab's dynasty was under a death sentence, but the execution had been delayed. God, in his staggering mercy, had given the king more time. The question was what Ahab would do with it. Would the man who tore his clothes in grief actually change the way he lived? Or would he go right back to ignoring God's word the next time it got in his way? The answer was coming—and it would arrive in the form of one honest prophet, four hundred liars, a disguise that couldn't fool God, and an arrow that found its target in a crowd of thousands.

Turn the page.

10

THE ARROW THAT COULDN'T MISS

In *The Hunger Games*, the Capitol rigs everything. The arena, the rules, the alliances, the cameras—it's all designed so the people in power stay in power and the odds are never really in your favor. But the thing about a rigged game is that it only works as long as you don't know it's rigged. The moment Katniss figures out the game, she starts making choices the Capitol didn't plan for.

First Kings 22 is the story of a rigged game, except the one doing the rigging isn't a corrupt government. It's God. And unlike Katniss, the man caught in the middle is told exactly how the game is set up. He's shown the trap, warned about the outcome, and given every chance to walk away.

He walks straight into it anyway.

This is the final chapter of Ahab's life, and it brings together everything the book of 1 Kings has been building toward: true prophets and false ones, the power of God's word, and the question of what happens to a king who refuses to listen.

THE PLAN

Three years of peace had passed between Israel and Aram since the battle at Aphek. During that time, Jehoshaphat king of Judah came to visit Ahab—a state visit between the two kingdoms. Jehoshaphat was a good king, a man who genuinely followed God. But he had made a terrible political decision: he had allied himself with Ahab through a marriage, giving his son Jehoram as husband to Ahab's daughter Athaliah. That marriage would nearly destroy the line of David a generation later. For now, though, it meant Jehoshaphat was stuck in Ahab's corner.

Ahab floated an idea to his advisors while Jehoshaphat was there: "Don't you know that Ramoth-gilead belongs to us? And yet we're doing nothing to take it back from the king of Aram." Ramoth-gilead was a strategically important city east of the Jordan River, sitting on a major trade route. Whoever controlled it collected the toll revenue. Aram had promised to return it after the last war but never did.

Ahab turned to Jehoshaphat: Will you go with me to fight for it?

Jehoshaphat answered with a pledge that went too far too fast: "I am as you are, my people as your people, my horses as your horses." He committed his entire kingdom before asking a single question about God's will. Then, almost as an afterthought, he added: "But first, let's seek the counsel of the LORD."

That request set off a chain of events that would expose the difference between what people want to hear and what God actually says.

FOUR HUNDRED TO ONE

Ahab gathered four hundred prophets—a number that should ring a bell. Back on Mount Carmel, four hundred prophets of Asherah had been invited but never showed up. Now four hundred prophets appear at Ahab's court, all claiming to speak for God. These weren't Baal prophets. They used God's name. They employed the classic prophetic formula: "This is what the LORD says." They looked and sounded like the real thing.

Ahab asked them the question: "Should I go to war against Ramoth-gilead, or should I hold back?" The answer was unanimous: "Go. The Lord will give it into the king's hand."

One of them, a prophet named Zedekiah, even put on a dramatic performance. He made iron horns and acted out Ahab goring the Arameans like a bull. He wasn't just making things up—he was actually quoting Scripture, applying a promise from Moses' blessing on the tribes of Joseph. He had the right formula, the right text, the right energy. All four hundred prophets agreed with him. It was a perfect consensus.

But Jehoshaphat wasn't convinced. Something felt off. "Is there not a prophet of the LORD here whom we can inquire of?" he asked. Notice the phrasing—he wanted a prophet of the Lord, implying the four hundred might not actually qualify.

Ahab's answer was revealing: "There is still one man through whom we can inquire of the LORD, but I hate him because he never prophesies anything good about me, but always bad. He is Micaiah son of Imlah."

Read that again. Ahab admitted there was a prophet who told the truth. He admitted that prophet was connected to God. And he hated the man for it. Ahab didn't evaluate prophets by whether they were right. He evaluated them by whether they were nice. A prophet who told him what he wanted to hear was a good prophet. A prophet who told him the truth was an enemy.

Jehoshaphat gently pushed back: "The king should not say that." So Ahab, reluctantly, sent for Micaiah.

THE PRESSURE AND THE PROPHET

While they waited for Micaiah, the scene at the gate of Samaria was impressive. Two kings sat on temporary thrones in full royal robes at the threshing floor outside the city gate. Four hundred prophets performed before them, prophesying victory, putting on dramatic displays. It was a pep rally with theological decorations.

The messenger sent to fetch Micaiah tried to coach him on the way: "Look, everyone else is prophesying success. Just agree with them. Don't make trouble." Micaiah's answer cut straight through: "As surely as the LORD lives, I can tell him only what the LORD tells me."

That single sentence captured something Ahab and his court never understood. The word of God is not under human control. A true prophet doesn't get to adjust the message depending on the audience. He doesn't soften it because it's inconvenient, inflate it because it's popular, or bend it because a king is listening. The word of God is a given, and the prophet's only job is to pass it along.

SARCASM AND TRUTH

When Micaiah arrived, Ahab asked the question: "Should we go to war against Ramoth-gilead, or not?"

Micaiah's first answer was surprising: "Attack and be victorious, for the LORD will give it into the king's hand." Word for word, he repeated what the four hundred had said.

But Ahab knew immediately it wasn't real. This had happened before—Micaiah had a habit of echoing the party line with obvious sarcasm before delivering the actual message. Ahab snapped at him: "How many times must I make you swear to tell me nothing but the truth in the name of the LORD?"

So Micaiah dropped the act: "I saw all Israel scattered on the hills like sheep without a shepherd, and the LORD said, 'These people have no master. Let each one go home in peace.'"

The meaning was unmistakable. If Israel has no shepherd, the shepherd is dead. Ahab would not survive this battle. And notice the bitter irony: when Ahab died, Israel would have peace. The "troubler of Israel"—Ahab's own label for Elijah—was actually Ahab himself.

Ahab turned to Jehoshaphat with a smug look: "Didn't I tell you? He never prophesies anything good about me."

But Micaiah wasn't finished.

THE THRONE ROOM BEHIND THE THRONE ROOM

What came next was the most remarkable vision in the entire book of 1 Kings. Micaiah described a scene from God's heavenly court—a council room far above and beyond the threshing floor where two earthly kings sat on their little thrones. "I saw the LORD sitting on his throne with all the armies of heaven standing around him on his right and on his left," Micaiah said. "And the LORD said, 'Who will entice Ahab into attacking Ramoth-gilead and going to his death there?'"

Various suggestions came from the heavenly court. Then a spirit stepped forward and said, "I will entice him by being a lying spirit in the mouths of all his prophets."

"You will succeed," the LORD said. "Go and do it."

Micaiah turned to Ahab and delivered the verdict plainly: "So now the LORD has put a lying spirit in the mouths of all these prophets of yours. The LORD has decreed disaster against you."

This is one of the most startling passages in the Bible, and it raises questions that have puzzled readers for thousands of years. But the main point is actually straightforward: God had decided that Ahab's time was up. Three prophets across three chapters had warned him. He had ignored every one. Now God was using Ahab's own preference for comfortable lies to lead him exactly where his judgment was waiting.

And here's the key detail that many people miss: there was no actual deception. God told Ahab, through Micaiah, exactly what was happening. He showed Ahab the trap before springing it. Ahab knew the four hundred were being used to lure him. He had been warned, plainly and publicly, that going to Ramoth-gilead meant death. God could not have been more transparent.

What would Ahab do with that information?

THE SLAP AND THE CELL

Before Ahab could respond, Zedekiah (the prophet with the iron horns) stepped up and slapped Micaiah across the face. "Which way did the spirit of the LORD go when he went from me to speak to you?" he sneered. In other words: I claim God's

Spirit too. How do you know you're right and I'm wrong?

Micaiah didn't argue. He simply said, "You will find out on the day you go to hide in an inner room"—implying that when disaster struck, Zedekiah would be running for cover.

Ahab had heard enough. He ordered Micaiah thrown in prison on bread and water until the king returned safely from battle. Micaiah's parting words were calm and devastating: "If you ever return safely, the LORD has not spoken through me. Mark my words, all you people."

The prophet of God was punished. The four hundred liars were celebrated. The true word was locked in a cell while the false word rode to war. That's what it looked like on the surface. But appearances are not the final word.

THE DISGUISE AND THE ARROW

Ahab went to Ramoth-gilead. But his behavior betrayed his fear. He told Jehoshaphat, "I will enter the battle in disguise, but you wear your royal robes." Think about what that means. If Micaiah was wrong, there was no danger—so why the disguise? And if Micaiah was right, no disguise could save him. Ahab was trapped in a contradiction of his own making: he rejected the prophet's word but couldn't stop being afraid of it.

Jehoshaphat, incredibly, agreed to this arrangement. He rode into battle dressed as a king while the actual king of Israel hid among his own soldiers. It was the ultimate expression of Ahab's character: passive, calculating, willing to let someone else take the hit.

The king of Aram had given his chariot commanders a single order: "Don't fight anyone except the king of Israel." When they spotted Jehoshaphat in his royal robes, they assumed he was Ahab and swarmed him. Jehoshaphat cried out, and the Arameans realized their mistake and broke off the pursuit. Jehoshaphat survived by a breath.

Meanwhile, buried in the chaos of battle, a nameless Aramean soldier—the text literally says "a man"—drew his bow at random and released an arrow into the crowd. That arrow flew through the chaos, past hundreds of soldiers, and struck the king of Israel in the one narrow gap between the sections of his armor.

Nobody aimed that shot. Nobody knew Ahab was there. A random arrow found the only vulnerable spot on a disguised king hiding in a crowd. The word of God doesn't need human planning to accomplish its purpose. It accomplishes it anyway—even "accidentally."

Ahab was propped up in his chariot facing the Arameans all day, blood pooling on the chariot floor. By evening he was dead. The army disbanded. The campaign was over. The chariot was washed at the pool of Samaria, and dogs licked up the king's blood—fulfilling what the prophet had spoken against him.

Three prophets had warned Ahab across three chapters. The unnamed prophet in chapter 20 had told him his life was forfeit. Elijah in chapter 21 had pronounced doom on his dynasty. Micaiah in chapter 22 had seen his death in a vision. Every word came true. Not because the prophets were lucky guessers, but because the God who spoke through them controls history down to the flight path of a single arrow.

WHAT THIS MEANS FOR US

First, hearing the truth isn't the same as following it. Ahab had access to the real word of God through Micaiah. He even demanded to hear it. But he treated it as a formality rather than a guide. Knowing what's right and doing what's right are two very different things.

Second, popularity doesn't equal truth. Four hundred prophets said one thing. One said another. The one was right. The size of the crowd agreeing with you has nothing to do with whether you're correct. Truth doesn't take a vote.

Third, you can't outsmart God's word. Ahab disguised himself, hid in the crowd, and took every precaution. A random arrow found him anyway. You can run from what God has said, but you cannot outrun it.

Fourth, true faithfulness is costly. Micaiah spoke the truth and got slapped in the face and thrown in prison. The four hundred told lies and received applause. Following God doesn't always come with rewards you can see right away. Sometimes it comes with a jail cell and stale bread.

Fifth, God's word is the only thing that lasts. The book of 1 Kings ends by mentioning Ahab's ivory palace and all the cities he built—impressive achievements that the biblical writer brushes past in a single verse. None of it mattered in the end. The only question that defined Ahab's legacy was this: How did he respond to the word of God? That's the question that defines everyone's legacy.

TALKING POINTS

1. **Ahab had four hundred prophets telling him what he wanted to hear and one telling him the truth.** How do you decide who to listen to when most people say one thing and one person says another?

2. **Micaiah used sarcasm before telling the truth, and Ahab recognized it immediately.** Why do you think Ahab wanted the truth but then ignored it?

3. **Ahab disguised himself to avoid the prophecy, but a random arrow found him.** What does that tell you about trying to avoid the consequences of your choices?

4. **Jehoshaphat was a good king who made a bad alliance.** What can happen when good people tie themselves too closely to people who don't share their values?

5. **The book of 1 Kings ends by listing Ahab's impressive buildings and then brushing past them.** What does that suggest about how God measures a person's life compared to how the world measures it?

Ahab was buried, and his son Ahaziah took the throne and walked in every evil his father and mother had practiced. The book of 1 Kings ends the way it began—with a kingdom waiting to see what kind of king it would get.

But by now, you know the answer. Every king in this book fell short. Solomon had all the wisdom in the world and still couldn't keep his own heart faithful. Rehoboam had a united kingdom handed to him and shattered it with a single speech. Jeroboam invented a counterfeit religion to hold onto power.

And Ahab—passive, spineless Ahab—sold himself to do evil because he never learned to say no.

The prophets were different. Elijah stood alone on a mountain and called an entire nation to choose. Micaiah told the truth to a king's face and accepted a prison cell for it. Unnamed prophets delivered God's word without asking for credit. These men didn't wear crowns, but they carried the only thing that mattered: the word of God. And that word was right every single time. It predicted the drought and the rain. It announced the fall of dynasties before the first sword was drawn. It found Ahab in a stolen vineyard and found him again on a battlefield, hiding in disguise. No one outran it. No one outlasted it.

That's the real story of 1 Kings. Not the rise and fall of kingdoms—though that's there. Not the miracles and battles—though those are unforgettable. The real story is that God's word never fails, and every human king does. The throne kept getting filled, and the man sitting on it kept getting it wrong. Wise kings turned foolish. Strong kings turned weak. Even the best of them couldn't stay faithful for a whole lifetime.

Which means 1 Kings leaves you with a question it never answers: Is there a king out there who won't fail? A king whose heart won't turn? A king who listens to God's word perfectly, not just on his good days but always?

Israel didn't have that king yet. They wouldn't for a long time. But the story wasn't over. The prophets were still speaking. The word was still going out. And centuries later, in a town not far from where Solomon's temple once gleamed on its hilltop, a baby would be born into the line of David—a King who would never bow to an idol, never ignore a prophet, never sell himself to do evil. A King whose kingdom would never split, never crumble, never end.

The whole book has been pointing to him. Every failed king made the Christ more necessary. Every faithful prophet made his coming more certain.

But that's the rest of the story. For now, the kingdom is divided, the throne is occupied by fools, and the prophets are still speaking into the darkness.

And God's word has not yet finished doing its work.

www.ingramcontent.com/pod-product-compliance
Ingram Content Group UK Ltd.
Pitfield, Milton Keynes, MK11 3LW, UK
UKHW020420250726
13967UKWH00007B/2733